DUNELAND
ELECTRIC

RAILROAD

101

Denny Hamilton

2

DUNELAND ELECTRIC

SOUTH SHORE LINE IN TRANSITION•DONALD R. KAPLAN

Photography by Donald R. Kaplan except as noted

Introduction................................ 6

1 Escape from the loop........................ 8

2 In the shadow of the mills 16

3 Duneland electric 32

4 Streetwise in Michigan City 48

5 Shops: genius department 60

6 Interurban time machine 72

7 From Pullman to Sumitomo............... 88

8 From Joes to Geeps 96

9 A new interurban era...................... 106

South Bend-bound train No. 469 climbs the embankment to cross the Baltimore & Ohio tracks at Miller, Ind., on the evening of March 27, 1982.
Cover photo (dustjacket on casebound books): The Saturday evening train out of South Bend for Chicago trails its own little whirling snowstorm on the prairies near Lydick, Ind., at the close of a frosty January day in 1972 (Mike Schafer).

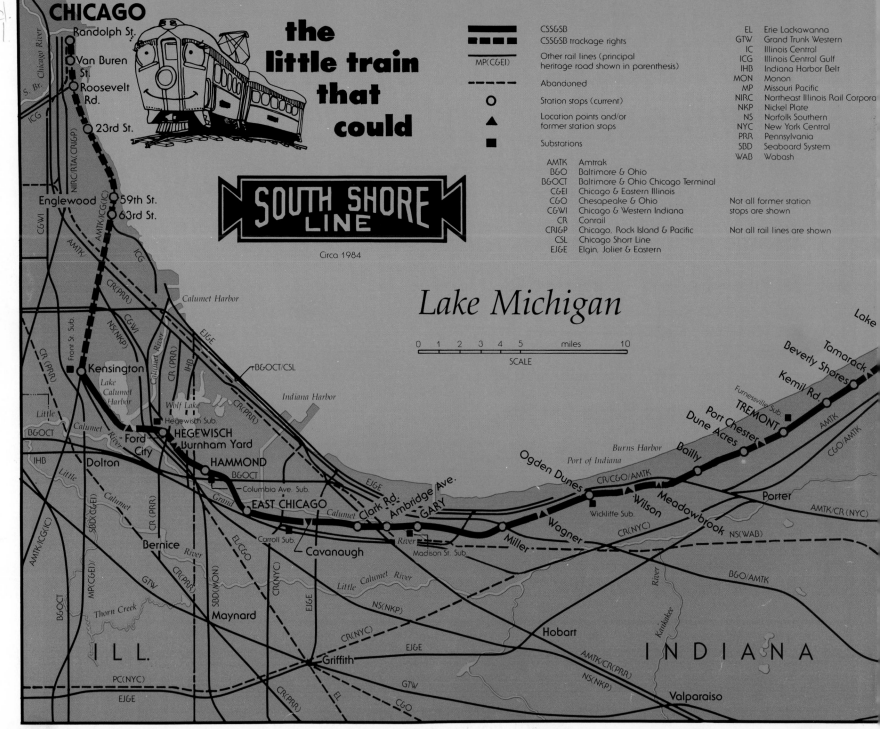

the
little train
that
could

SOUTH SHORE LINE

Circa 1984

CHICAGO

Randolph St.
Van Buren St.
Roosevelt Rd.
23rd St.
Englewood
59th St.
63rd St.

		CSS&SB
		CSS&SB trackage rights
MP(C&EI)		Other rail lines (principal heritage road shown in parentheses)
		Abandoned
○		Station stops (current)
▲		Location points and/or former station stops
■		Substations

AMTK   Amtrak
B&O   Baltimore & Ohio
B&OCT   Baltimore & Ohio Chicago Terminal
C&EI   Chicago & Eastern Illinois
C&O   Chesapeake & Ohio
C&WI   Chicago & Western Indiana
CR   Conrail
CRI&P   Chicago, Rock Island & Pacific
CSL   Chicago Short Line
EJ&E   Elgin, Joliet & Eastern

EL   Erie Lackawanna
GTW   Grand Trunk Western
IC   Illinois Central
ICG   Illinois Central Gulf
IHB   Indiana Harbor Belt
MON   Monon
MP   Missouri Pacific
NIRC   Northeast Illinois Rail Corpora
NKP   Nickel Plate
NS   Norfolk Southern
NYC   New York Central
PRR   Pennsylvania
SBD   Seaboard System
WAB   Wabash

Not all former station stops are shown

Not all rail lines are shown

Lake Michigan

| 0 | 1 | 2 | 3 | 4 | 5 | miles | 10 |
SCALE

Calumet Harbor

Indiana Harbor

B&OCT/CSL

Kensington
Lake Calumet Harbor
Wolf Lake
Hegewisch Sub.
HEGEWISCH
Ford City
Burnham Yard
HAMMOND
B&OCT
Dolton
Columbia Ave. Sub.
Carroll Sub.
EAST CHICAGO
Cavanaugh
Madison St. Sub.
Bernice
Grand
Calumet
River
Clark Rd.
Ambridge Ave.
GARY
Miller
River
Wickliffe Sub.
Ogden Dunes
Port of Indiana
Burns Harbor
CR/C&O/AMTK
Wagner
Wilson
Meadowbrook
Bailly
Dune Acres
Port Chester
TREMONT
Furnessville Sub.
Kemil Rd.
Beverly Shores
Tamarack
Lake
Porter

Maynard
Thorn Creek
Little Calumet River
Hobart
Kankakee River
I N D I A N A

I L L.
Griffith
Valparaiso

Little Calumet River

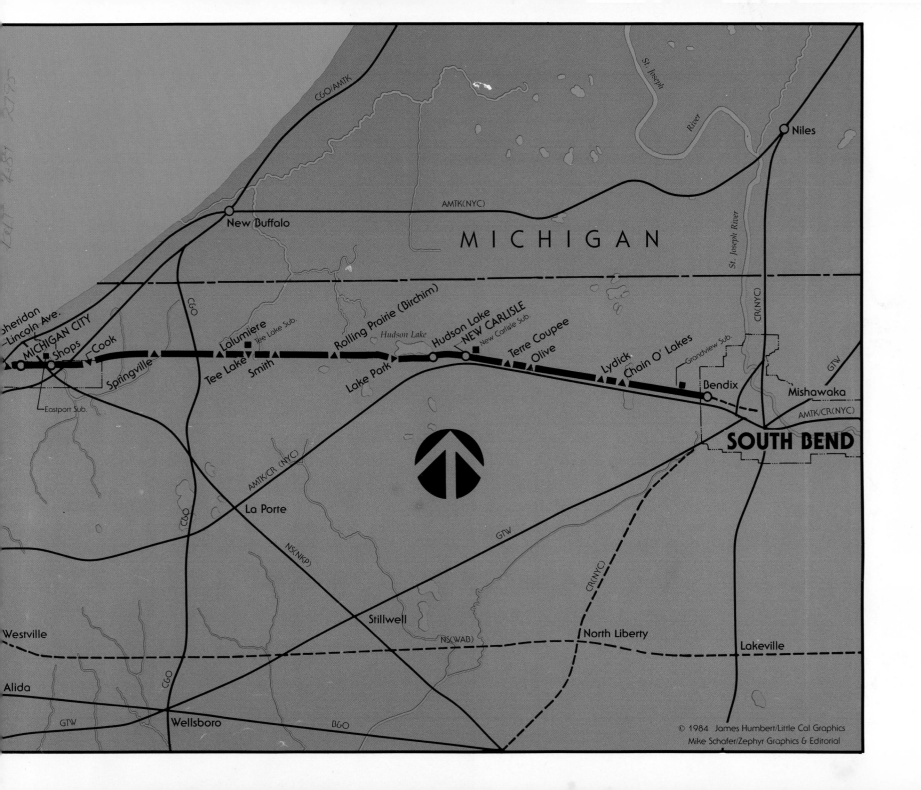

Niles

St. Joseph River

MICHIGAN

AMTK(NYC)

St. Joseph River

New Buffalo

CGO/AMTK

CGO

CR(NYC)

Sheridan
Lincoln Ave.

MICHIGAN CITY

Shops

Cook

Lalumiere

Rolling Prairie (Birchim)

Hudson Lake

NEW CARLISLE

Tee Lake Sub.

Hudson Lake

New Carlisle Sub.

Terre Coupee

Olive

Chain O' Lakes

Grandview Sub.

GTW

Tee Lake

Smith

Lake Park

Lydick

Bendix

Springville

Mishawaka

Eastport Sub.

AMTK/CR (NYC)

SOUTH BEND

CGO

AMTK/CR (NYC)

La Porte

GTW

CR(NYC)

NS(NKP)

Stillwell

NS(WAB)

North Liberty

Lakeville

Westville

CGO

Alida

GTW

Wellsboro

B&O

© 1984 James Humbert/Little Cal Graphics
Mike Schafer/Zephyr Graphics & Editorial

Above: Michigan City train 267 races the motorists on the Indiana Toll Road as it bounds downgrade on the East Chicago bypass near milepost 65 in August 1982. Right: A new generation of equipment reigns on the last interurban as train 309 approaches Hudson Lake station on a Sunday evening in June 1984.

Introduction

In the annals of American public transportation, the interurban electric railway was unique. For a rail system as extensive (16,100 miles) and as widespread as it became, it experienced the shortest boom (from about 1895 to 1915) and the most precipitous decline of any transport mode in the United States. By the end of the Great Depression, the vast majority of properties had been abandoned and only those few interurbans that developed a healthy carload freight business and achieved some integration into the nation's railroad system were able to survive into the postwar period.

The interurban was the rural offspring of the street railway systems that developed in municipalities prior to the turn of the century. A hybrid between a local trolley and a steam road-type train, the interurban's passenger rolling stock characteristically was larger, faster and more comfortable than that of its street railway cousins. But while the interurbans usually had a private right-of-way in the country, they depended upon street railway trackage for access to major cities and towns. For many of the systems such extensive amounts of street running, with tight curvature and clearances, was an impediment to the development of extensive freight services. The extent to which these companies mixed motormen and motorists meant the difference between survival and failure when competition from automobiles and buses became keen in the 1920's. It was only on the more heavily constructed interurbans that enough freight revenues could be developed to prop up failing passenger services during the lean years of the Depression.

The pinnacle of the interurban was represented by the trio of Insull-controlled lines radiating from the Chicago area: the Chicago Aurora and Elgin, the Chicago North Shore and Milwaukee and the Chicago South Shore and South Bend. Prior to their integration into Samuel Insull's Midwestern electric power and traction empire in the 1910's and 1920's, each had been a typical interurban property, with some of the shortcomings and poor performance standards of the industry. Following their incorporation into Insull's Midland Utilities Corp., however, the three lines were literally transformed into high-speed passenger systems with an infrastructure comparable to that of many steam railroads. The lines refurbished their physical plants and purchased high-speed passenger rolling stock that offered effective competition to railroad, automotive and bus traffic. The Insull management also aggressively pursued carload freight business and interchanges with steam railroads that would be critical to the survival of all three systems. As a result, all three of the Insull lines were able to survive the Depression with varying degrees of success. They later benefited from the tremendous boom in wartime traffic that permitted the postwar transition to modern, commuter networks serving the city of Chicago.

Of the three Insull super-interurbans, only the South Shore Line has managed to survive into today's era of federal and state subsidies. With a stronger financial position, both the CA&E and the North Shore, abandoned in 1957-61 and 1963 respectively, might also have made it into the subsidy era and experienced similar renaissance. Why, then, did the South Shore make it?

Among the primary factors are (1) the high quality of construction of South Shore basic right-of-way and the fact that street trackage in East Chicago, Michigan City and South Bend was devoid of the sharp curvature that would have prevented the movement of conventional railroad freight traffic; (2) the railroad's location in one of the industrial centers of the nation, the Calumet district at the southern tip of Lake Michigan; (3) the management's aggressive solicitation of carload freight traffic on a nationwide basis; (4) the Insull management's complete re-equipment of the South Shore's passenger fleet with heavy steel cars that could be altered and served for over 50 years despite the rigors of weather extremes around Lake Michigan; and (5) the railroad's access to the finest high speed entrance into the Chicago Loop via the electrified commuter lines of the Illinois Central.

While both North Shore and Aurora and Elgin did develop some carload freight business, those levels paled in comparison with that of the South Shore because the former's rails did not serve heavy industrial developments. Moreover, while both the CA&E and the North Shore did reach Chicago's loop via branches of the Chicago "L," the extreme curvature of elevated trackage not only slowed their trains but also placed marked restrictions on the dimensions of cars, limiting passenger capacities. By contrast, Illinois Central's electrified commuter right-of-way not only provided a more rapid penetration of the Loop than the the the rapid transit system but also could accommodate the larger rolling stock of the South Shore because the IC trackage was designed to steam-road specifications. Moreover, in the absence of weight and curvature restrictions, the South Shore was able to lengthen its passenger coaches in the 1940's in order to increase seating capacity, something that could never have been done on the CA&E or North Shore.

As the last interurban electric railway operating in the U.S., the South Shore line has undergone significant changes in its operations and its image in years from 1974 through 1984. Not only has its passenger service become more commuter oriented and modernized with new equipment from Japan but the image of the freight service has been altered markedly since the railroad became part of the larger Chessie System in 1967. In the past decade, the South Shore has shifted from general merchandise freight to an emphasis on bulk commodities in unit trains. The company gradually phased out electrified freight motive power in favor of more flexible diesel units.

In DUNELAND ELECTRIC, we highlight pictorially this decade of change in the last interurban's history, and salute the classic interurban image that has typified the railroad for most of its history. First, we make a geographic survey of the line and its facilities. As with any rail system that extends some distance from a major urban center into the country, the image of the South Shore and its function varies significantly along its route. A basic understanding of the railroad can best be achieved by examining its image from one end of the system to the other. We also want to assess, in some detail, how the South Shore has changed in this past decade using two specific markers of that change, passenger rolling stock and freight services and motive power. Finally, we chronicle the public activity that led to the rescue of the passenger service, and offer a prognosis now that the railroad has been refurbished.

Donald R. Kaplan
Kensington, Calif.
September 1984

A light snowfall softens the rough surfaces of the South Shore's ramshackle station at Randolph St. in Chicago.

Lou Gerard

1 Escape from the Loop

A major factor in the longevity of the South Shore line as a passenger carrier has been its access to downtown Chicago over the grade-separated, high-speed right-of-way of the Illinois Central Gulf electrified commuter route. Starting from its terminus at Randolph St., ICG rails run south-southeast parallel to the shore of Lake Michigan before turning inland in a more southwesterly direction at 51st St. South Shore trains depart the ICG main at Kensington, 115th St., 14.2 miles south of city center.

Throughout its history, the South Shore has used the Illinois Central as a gateway to downtown. From 1909 to 1911 the connection was made simply by the transfer of passengers to IC commuter trains, initially at Pullman (111th St.) and later at Kensington (115th St.). A significant improvement came in 1912 when coaches from certain Chicago Lake Shore & South Bend Railway (the South Shore's predecessor) trains were pulled by IC locomotives into Chicago. Finally, the South Shore's conversion in 1926 from the 6600-volt a.c. system of the Lake Shore to the 1500-volt d.c. system in use on the newly electrified IC led to a trackage rights agreement, enabling South Shore multiple-unit (m.u.) trains to run all the way into downtown Chicago under their own power.

South Shore trains begin and terminate their runs in Chicago at ICG's suburban commuter terminal at Randolph St. and Michigan Ave., one block east of the Chicago Loop. Both ICG and South Shore share a common subterranean waiting room with ticket facilities, but South Shore's rail terminal is spatially separated from that of the ICG. Approaching Randolph St. from the south, South Shore trains stay to the east and climb to an open-air stub track station, whereas ICG trains drop down a slight grade and dive into the subway terminal to the west.

The South Shore facility at Randolph St. consists of five tracks served by three high-level platforms. Except for rush hours when all five are used, only two of the older tracks are used for arrivals and departures during the day; the others are used for car storage, particularly during the day. In addition, trainmen and carmen offices occupy an adjacent building.

South of Randolph St., the ICG right-of-way is below street level as far as 43rd St., where it becomes elevated. Three electrified tracks run from the throat of the Ran-

dolph St. terminal to 11th Place and expand to four tracks to 113th St., where they again narrow to two tracks for the remainder of the ICG route. Between 11th Place and 113th, South Shore trains generally use the outermost express tracks (Nos. 1 and 4), where they can pass slower RTA locals that make intermediate station stops. Between Randolph and 11th Place, all trains are restricted to 20 mph. From 11th Place to 95th St. the speed limit is 50 mph and 70 mph from 95th to 115th St.

Throughout ICG suburban territory, stations have high-level platforms for rapid loading and unloading. All South Shore trains stop at Van Buren St., 12th St./Roosevelt Rd., 59th St. and 115th St./Kensington. Some trains also stop at 23rd and 63rd Sts.

Reduced maintenance during the 1970's caused ICG to deteriorate, providing a fairly rough ride for the older South Shore cars. However, as a result of an Illinois RTA-funded rail rehabilitation program in the late 1970's, ICG trackage has been improved to the point that the ride is almost as smooth as that along the South Shore.

Car 26 leads train 121 at Randolph St. In the background are the Prudential Building (left) and the Standard Oil of Indiana Building.

Randolph St. station is a place to buy sunglasses, read newspapers, shop for flowers or board trains. Ticket agent Sandra Johns handles phone inquiries behind the South Shore window.

Train 216 from Gary climbs a short grade under Monroe St. that leads into Randolph St. terminal.

The rear brakeman is ready to give the highball from the end of South Bend-bound train 81.

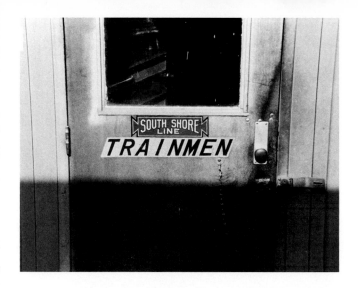

Brakeman-collector Steve Cox (right) announces the boarding of train 25 for South Bend. The trainmen's room at Randolph St. is clearly marked.

A carman supervises the coupling of cars 1 and 103.

Conductor R. "Foxy" Shires, reporting the arrival of train 118, calls from the trainmen's room at Randolph St.

A quartet of unmodernized Pullman cars heads north along Chicago's lakefront, passing the R. R. Donnelly & Sons Co. printing plant at 21st St.

Ed De Rouin

South Shore train 468 from South Bend cruises along newly rebuilt Illinois Central Gulf trackage near 35th St. on Chicago's South Side.

A long South Shore train rumbles across the ICG main line as it approaches Kensington station at 115th St. in November 1978.

Don Ellison

A two-car Gary train works its way through the interlocking plant at 115th St. as it heads onto Kensington & Eastern trackage in June 1978.

An eastbound train crosses the Calumet River, clogged with ice during the bitter cold of January 1981.

Mike Sc

Don Ellison

In the shadow of the mills

After departing the Illinois Central Gulf main line at 115th St., South Shore rails course 16.8 miles to Gary through the heart of the heavily industrial Calumet district. This urban-industrial complex just south and east of Chicago supplies the South Shore with most of its commuters and, at one time, a significant amount of its freight traffic.

Serving the Calumet region is a concentrated rail gridwork that the South Shore must intersect on its way east to Gary. It is in this busy Calumet sector the railroad reveals its true interurban nature. For example, of the nine railway lines it encounters, only two are crossed at grade; the other seven are crossed by overhead construction in true interurban style, with short but steep momentum grades.

One might assume that once South Shore trains leave the ICG at Kensington, they have reached their own right-of-way. Technically, however, South Shore trackage begins at State Line, Hammond, Ind., 6.4 miles to the south and east. From 115th St. to the Indiana line, South Shore trains traverse the Kensington & Eastern Railroad (K&E), an Illinois Central Gulf subsidiary completed in 1909 as a link between the South Shore's own track in Indiana and the IC main line at 111th St. According to the original Lake Shore franchise, the interurban line was incorporated strictly as an Indiana prop-

erty and was not allowed to build into Illinois. Since its completion, the Kensington & Eastern has been under perpetual lease to the South Shore, which is not only responsible for all the trackage and its maintenance but also pays taxes on the property. An Illinois Central Gulf freight transfer occasionally uses a portion of this K&E trackage to reach the Lake Calumet Harbor deepwater port of Chicago.

The 16.8 miles from 115th St. to Broadway station in Gary is double track with 13 crossovers along the route. Heading southeast, the tracks drop down a 1.6 percent grade from the elevated ICG main. At 130th St. the tracks curve east, climbing an 0.75 percent grade onto an embankment that carries them over Interstate 94, a branch of the Calumet River and the rails of the Norfolk Southern and Chicago & Western Indiana at Ford City (130th and Torrence Ave.).

After taking the Ford City curve southeast, the rails descend a 1 percent grade back to ground level at Hegewisch, the most important commuter stop in Illinois. A half-mile southeast of Hegewisch station, the rails pass Burnham Yard, South Shore's major freight facility in the Calumet District. At one time or another, the South Shore interchanged freight with the Norfolk & Western (former Nickel Plate), Chesapeake & Ohio, Belt Railway of Chicago, Louisville & Nashville (former Monon),

Erie Lackawanna (former Erie), Chicago & Western Indiana and Indiana Harbor Belt at Burnham. At the east end of Burnham Yard, South Shore trains cross the IHB at grade through State Line interlocking—once one of the largest mechanical interlockings in the U.S.—and enter their own trackage at State Line about 40 feet east of the Indiana Harbor Belt diamond.

At State Line curve the tracks turn east past South Shore's Burnham Yard freight office and run through the backyards of residential Hammond. Beyond Hammond station at Hohman Ave. they continue their backyard route, crossing several streets at grade before climbing a 2.7 percent grade to enter the five-mile stretch of grade-separated route of the East Chicago Bypass that takes South Shore trains through the peripheries of Hammond and East Chicago.

Prior to completion of the bypass in September 1956, South Shore trains stayed at ground level, crossed the Baltimore & Ohio Chicago Terminal at grade and penetrated downtown East Chicago via two miles of street running on Chicago Ave. Heavy automobile and truck traffic, numerous railroad crossings at grade and traffic lights slowed the South Shore trains.

The headache of East Chicago street running was recognized soon after the road's takeover by Insull management in the late 1920's. As early as 1927, South

Shore acquired property to build such a bypass route, but litigation delayed its startup until the early 1930's. By that time the railroad was struggling through the Depression and could not afford the capital expenditure for construction, and more than a quarter century passed before the bypass was built. Ultimately, South Shore's property was deeded to the Indiana Toll Road Commission and joint construction of the parallel Interstate 90-94 toll road and new South Shore route commenced in 1954. Ironically, while South Shore managed to eliminate its East Chicago bottleneck, it also helped provide a new roadway for its automotive competition.

After climbing the grade along the freight lead to the B&OCT interchange, the bypass route turns southeast at Columbia Ave., Hammond and then heads in a southeasterly direction for over 2 miles before turning east again just west of East Chicago station. Through this portion of the bypass the rails are on an embankment, and the East Chicago station is on two levels, with a ground-level waiting room and ticket booth and rail-level platforms. A mile east of the station the bypass returns to ground level.

At Cline Ave., the western limit of Gary, the South Shore tracks pass under a rail girder and highway bridge (Cline Ave.) which carries a South Shore freight lead up and over both the South Shore main and the toll road to serve the Harbison-Walker Refractory plant in an industrial park on the north side of the toll road. The eastern boundary of the East Chicago bypass is just east of Cline Ave., at the former stop called Cavanaugh. At this point the original main line that ran southeast from its Chicago Ave. street running turned east. East of Cavanaugh the South Shore rails make one of their most abrupt grades (3.2 percent) to cross the Elgin Joliet & Eastern. About a mile and a half farther east is Clark Road, the major flag stop on the west side of Gary. Like the other flag stop in Gary (Ambridge), Clark Road is furnished with a simple wooden shelter painted traction orange.

Just east of Clark Road the rails duck under highway U.S. 12 and climb a short 2.5 percent grade to a double span, truss-type gantlet bridge (two sets of rails laid on a roadbed of single-track width) which crosses over the tracks of Conrail (former Pennsylvania) and Norfolk Southern (former Wabash). Dropping down the 2.5 percent grade east of the bridge, the South Shore tracks run past the former NS interchange and Georgia Pacific paper mill that still is serviced by the South Shore. From Ambridge east to Gary, Broadway station, South Shore

Chicago-bound train 212 races toward the Calumet River bridge in March 1983.

track occupies a broad median at ground level between Third Ave. and 2nd Place. Part of the greater width of the right-of-way here is to accommodate 0.7-mile-long Marshall siding, which extends from Grant to Marshall streets between the east and westbound mains.

The main station in downtown Gary at Broadway St. dated back to the original Lake Shore days. It differed from all other passenger facilities on the railroad in having high-level platforms as well as two stub tracks at the west end of the station, between the east and westbound mains. In addition to being an agency station with a waiting room, Gary also had a waiting room for crew and carmen.

Until 1983 there was a four-track coach yard just west of Gary station. However, because of vandalism, cars now are stored at Michigan City Shops (nights and

weekends) and at Randolph St. (weekdays). Since there was little need for this yard, its tracks were taken up.

The entire original Gary station was replaced in June 1984 as part of a one-mile line change between Harrison and Virginia streets. The new tracks are on a contained fill that crosses Broadway on a bridge. The ticket office will be located in a new Gary Public Transportation Center that will serve local and intercity bus passengers as well as South Shore riders. Relocation of the South Shore right-of-way is part of the construction of the Broadway interchange of the Indiana Toll Road.

Five substations supply the busy Kensington-Gary section of the South Shore with power: Front St. (ICG), Kensington; Hegewisch (new); Columbia Ave., Hammond; Carroll, Hammond; and Madison St. just west of the present Gary station.

Clockwise from above: A trio of old cars traces the Ford City curve just west of Hegewisch station; coming off the curve, a train drops down a 1 percent grade into Hegewisch; the crew in Little Joe 802 had this view of a pans-down, coasting train 276 at Ford City in June 1979.

Hegewisch passengers board from a sturdy brick station.

Soda pop, SUN TIMES and suburban trains.

The Hegewisch waiting room mixes passengers, news vendor and ticket agent.

Two women disembark an eastbound train at Hegewisch.

The order hoops are empty as train 284 rounds State Line curve in Hammond and passes the South Shore freight depot.

After easing through State Line curve, South Shore trains slip into Hammond station on Hohman Ave. on the city's north side.

Don Ellison

Mike Schafer

Commuters and shoppers have friends to meet, cabs to call and trains to catch at Hohman Ave. in Hammond, all under the watchful gaze of smartly uniformed South Shore trainmen.

The Hammond station waiting room is nearly empty on this June 1984 afternoon as a pair of passengers await train 114.

Train 213 hits the Calumet crossover as it climbs the 2.7 percent grade to the East Chicago bypass.

East Chicago passengers meet South Shore trains at the elevated station above Indianapolis Blvd.

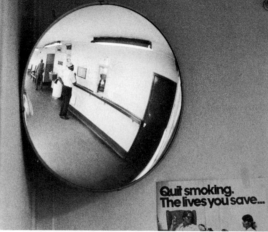

A visual annunciator warns of an east-bound train at East Chicago as passengers of all shapes and sizes purchase tickets in the ground-level waiting room. Between trains, an agent reads the morning paper.

Preceding page, clockwise from far left: Train 168 slips through the Clark Crossover in Gary; passengers get a peek at a cartoon character as their train hits the 3.2 percent grade coming off the bridge over the Elgin, Joliet & Eastern; a six-car Sumitomo trainset crosses Conrail (foreground) and Norfolk & Western via a double-span gantlet bridge.

Ed De Rouin

Don Ellison

Above: A Little Joe and an eastbound train congregate at Gary on a March 1977 evening. Left: A South Shore train overpasses a Baltimore & Ohio train at Hammond. Far left: At Gary, the old station sign was just as interesting as the trains.

Ed De Rouin

29

Don Ellison

Left to right: Train 261 kicks up the snow at the Ambridge stop in January 1978; three passengers step out of the Clark Rd. shelter to board a Chicago-bound train in western Gary; at Gary, riders step onto the only South Shore high-level platforms outside the Illinois Central Gulf portion of the route.

Steam from the Bethlehem Steel plant at Burns Harbor climbs lazily into a July 1978 sky as a westbound train vaults the Conrail main line.

Tom Post

Denny Hamilton

3

Duneland electric

The central segment of the South Shore from Gary station to the main station in Michigan City is 24.9 miles long. Here the railroad runs through the heart of the Indiana sand dunes region, paralleling the southern shore of Lake Michigan a mile to a mile and a half south of the shoreline.

In contrast to the urban-industrial character of the Calumet District, the territory east of Gary is more suburban to rural. Many commuters board at stations such as Miller, Ogden Dunes and Dune Acres. Along the less industrialized portions of the route, the rails pass through forested sand dunes that provide a scenic ride. Except for overpasses over the Baltimore & Ohio at Miller, Conrail just west of the Bailly stop and over the entrance to Bethlehem Steel, there are no sharp curves or significant changes of grade.

About halfway along the route, the otherwise bucolic duneland image is interrupted by a large industrial complex in the Burns Harbor area dominated by the huge Bethlehem Steel and Midwest Steel plants. South Shore currently does the majority of its freight business hauling coal and equipment to Bethlehem Steel, and coal to the Bailly and Michigan City power plants of the Northern Indiana Public Service Company (NIPSCO).

Passenger traffic is considerably lighter in this central sector than in the Calumet region. With passenger train frequency cut in half, there isn't the need for much double track, and double track ends at Tennessee St., 1.1 mile east of Gary station. Provision for train meets along the central zone is by three long high-speed passing sidings furnished with spring switches and long (No. 20) turnouts (1.2-mile Wagner siding east of Miller, 2.7-mile Wilson siding west of Bailly, and 0.7-mile Tamarack siding), which are operated as double track for high-speed meets. Although the intervening portions of the route are single track, the right-of-way was designed to be double-tracked along its length; alternating-beam catenary supports span the width of two tracks. The railroad never completed double tracking the central region, and by the time it could have been done, traffic did not warrant more than one track. The present system of single track and ample passing sidings more than accommodates current traffic.

Heading east from Broadway station, South Shore parallels U.S. 12-20—so close, in fact, especially in the vicinity of Aetna on Gary's east side, that it resembles a side-of-the-road trolley. In this section just east of Gary station the railroad retains some of its industrial image. In addition to crossing a branch of the EJ&E at grade there is the Gary team track (or "flour track"), where Conagra Corp. siphons flour from hoppers. Just east is Goff Junction, where the South Shore interchanges

miscellaneous freight with the EJ&E.

Further east—3.9 miles from Gary station—is Miller station, an important stop on Gary's east side and also a significant interchange point with parent Chessie (B&O), especially for unit coal trains. Departing Miller station, the rails immediately climb a 2.5 percent grade to cross the B&O on a single-span truss bridge and descend another 2.5 percent grade to ground level. Just east of the B&O crossing is Wagner double track with its distinctive, all-steel catenary bridges. When first refurbished by Insull management in 1926, this siding was called the "Ideal Section" and was to be a showcase for the kind of catenary support to be installed on all parts of the railroad. Instead, the remainder of the catenary is supported either by laced steel portal beams mounted between two wooden poles or by single wooden poles with mast arms.

Two miles beyond Wagner is the important commuter stop of Ogden Dunes, which also is the site of Wickliffe Substation, one of two substations along this portion of the route. The other is Furnessville sub, 1.1 mile east of Tremont. Three quarters of a mile east of Ogden Dunes marks the beginning of Wilson double track, the longest passing siding on the railroad. At the east end of Wilson, near the site of the former Meadowbrook stop, the rails climb a 1 percent grade, round a curve northeast and cross a girder bridge over the relocated former New York Central (now Conrail) main line. Beyond, the tracks cross a single-span truss bridge originally built to carry the South Shore over the NYC, and what now is the main entrance road to Bethlehem Steel. From these overpasses the track descends a 1.5 percent grade to pass Bailly station at the east entrance to the steel plant.

From Bailly east, South Shore rails again pass through the sandy territory that has been preserved as part of the Indiana Dunes National Lakeshore. Having left most traces of greater Chicago's urban sprawl, the solitary track skirts attractive homes and old motels scattered through the wooded dunes along U.S. 12.

Even some of the station structures take on a greater charm as the tracks head east. Virtually all the major stops (Miller, Ogden Dunes, Bailly, Dune Acres and Tremont) are now served only by small, orange, wooden shelters. Beverly Shores, however, has a quaint, Spanish-style tile-roofed stucco station constructed by Insull management in the late 1920's. This combination agency-home station is architecturally identical to those built along the North Shore Line's Skokie Valley Route in 1926. Today the Beverly Shores station is occupied as a private home, while the waiting room still functions as a passenger shelter.

After passing through the wooded community of Pines, the South Shore rails pass from Porter into La Porte County and enter the limits of Michigan City. At the west side of Michigan City the rails pass the Power Siding lead that takes South Shore unit trains to NIPSCO's gigantic Michigan City generating station and adjacent Lincoln Yard, where an interchange with Conrail can still be made. Beyond the power lead, the rails turn east and pass 0.1-mile-long Sheridan siding, a typical meeting point for trains into and out of Michigan City, the South Shore's home and center of operations.

Train 112 pauses next to a string of Chessie coil cars as it picks up riders at Miller on Gary's east side.

An icicle-equipped eastbound train climbs the grade to the B&OCT crossing at Miller in January 1978.

A South Shore train meets a pair of Chessie System locomotives running light at Miller.

Don Ellison

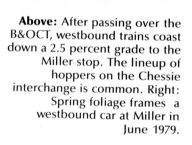

Above: After passing over the B&OCT, westbound trains coast down a 2.5 percent grade to the Miller stop. The lineup of hoppers on the Chessie interchange is common. Right: Spring foliage frames a westbound car at Miller in June 1979.

Chuck Crouse

Preceding page: The steel catenary supports of the "Ideal Section" form a tunnel for train 402 at Wagner siding in June 1984. Left: A Sunday-afternoon sun catches the flanks of an eastbound train at Bailly in March 1982. Above: Electric power on display at Bailly.

39

Train 77, South Shore's fastest, sprints past
the steel mills in Burns Harbor on its way to
South Bend on an August 1982 evening.

Dune Acres is a stop patronized mostly by affluent commuters who live in the Indiana duneland north of the South Shore. In the photo at left, passengers board a bus to be transported around track work being performed in August 1979.

Chuck Crouse

An orange shelter protects passengers at the dunes-area stop called Tremont, where collector Greg Jeanes (above) beckons riders from the platform vestibule of train 114.

Light snow flurries won't slow a westbound train as it slips through the siding at Tremont in late March 1982.

Above: Always the interurban—a South Shore train speeds past Furnessville substation. Left: A new generation of equipment passes the since-razed Insull-era Lake Shore station in Pines, March 1983.

The wind is coming off Lake Michigan, and that means snow as a westbound pair of Pullmans rolls through Pines in March 1982. Left: A westbound train takes the turnout at the east end of Tamarack siding, as framed in the engineer's window aboard GP38-2 No. 2001, running as a cab hop back to Shops in March 1982.

45

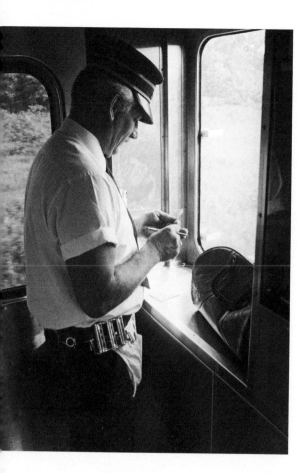

Left: A Chicago-bound train crosses U.S. 12 on Michigan City's west side. Above: Conductor Mike Thomas counts fares as train 118 rushes through the dunes region. Right: Train 115 is framed in the front platform window of a Sumitomo car at Sheridan in Michigan City.

A pair of old cars heads for Shops as the t[...]
trundles down 11th St. at Lafayette in
Michigan City in September 1979.

Mike Schafer

4 Streetwise in Michigan City

I f in its rolling stock and right-of-way today's South Shore Line bears little resemblance to interurbans of the past, the railroad's route and facilities in Michigan City reveal a traction heritage. In classic interurban fashion, South Shore trains reach downtown Michigan City via two miles of street running down the middle of 10th and 11th streets, including a station stop at a classic storefront depot at 11th near Franklin St. Prior to 1956, South Shore trains ran through the streets in three communities: East Chicago, Michigan City and South Bend. Street running in East Chicago was eliminated in September 1956, and removed in South Bend in the 1970's, when the line was cut back two miles to the Bendix stop, leaving Michigan City as the last expression of an interurban trait.

Beginning at the intersection of Sheridan Ave. and 10th St., South Shore trains run east down the center of 10th St. After crossing the former Michigan Central (now Amtrak) main at grade at Huron St., the line takes a reverse curve to swing over to 11th St. upon which

it operates east to the main station at Franklin. From Franklin the rails head east for three blocks before dropping down a 2.4 percent grade as they sweep through an impressive reverse curve on 11th between Cedar and Lafayette streets. From Lafayette they climb another 2.4 percent grade cresting at Oak St. before descending a 1.4 percent grade to the end of street running at East Michigan Blvd. (U.S. 35).

Despite its interurban roots, street running in Michigan City is in its operation and construction more akin to mainline railroading. Although the route is hilly, there is none of the tight curvature that typified interurban lines through cities. Furthermore, the line is block signaled right through town, with color-light signals mounted at curbside. Metal crossbucks guard intersections in addition to crossing flashers at transitions between street running and private right-of-way and at Willard Ave., where some trains stop to pick up and discharge passengers in the middle of the street. Moreover, street trackage is heavy-duty (115 lb.), welded rail

planked along its entire length to provide for the depth of conventional rail wheel flanges as well as a relatively smooth surface for vehicular traffic. Even the traffic signals at the intersections of 11th St. with Franklin, Washington and Wabash streets are interconnected with track circuits so they will not be an impediment to train movement. Once the signals have changed to green for 11th St. and a train is in the circuit, the lights will be held green for the train. Pairs of flashing white light bulbs mounted on line poles both east and west of Michigan City's main station indicate to the engineer that the traffic signals are lined for the train.

Michigan City's other traction remnant is the classic storefront station downtown. Originally opened in May 1927, this handsome two-story terra cotta building served as a combination rail-motor coach facility. Buses of the railroad's subsidiary Shore Line Motor Coach Co. connected with trains at Michigan City to provide transportation to lakeside Michigan communities such as Bridgman, St. Joseph and Benton Harbor. In its hey-

In the sequence above, train 468 (above) has just come off street running at 10th St. and switched onto the passing track at Sheridan siding. No. 468 passes train 361 (center) about midway along the siding. Westbound 468 regains the main line (far right) as 361 continues its trip east on this August 1981 afternoon.

day, Michigan City station offered a full range of amenities, including a large waiting room, lunch counter, large ticket and information booth as well as separate parcel and baggage rooms. An ample brick bus garage extended from the main station building to Pine St. on the east.

Today's station is a ghost. The bus garage has been razed for parking spaces, but the building exterior is relatively unchanged. The interior, however, has been radically altered. The ticket agent on duty weekday mornings occupies a small office at the rear of the building, leaving the original ticket-information booth empty for storage. Similarly, all that remains of the amenities are the waiting room, with its benches, plus a gong and light indicators signaling the arrival of a train and its direction of travel. Amid financial constraint in the 1960's and 1970's, most of the railroad's passenger fa-

cilities were cut to the bone. Michigan City's once splendid station today stands as a testament to such economic measures, and as of press time, plans are afoot to tear it down and replace it with a more modest facility.

In addition to the main station in the center of town and the grocery store/street stop at Willard Ave., Shops is the third station stop in Michigan City. After proceeding back onto private right-of-way east of Michigan Blvd., South Shore tracks make a reverse curve and head straight east parallel to Holliday St., dropping down a 1.5 percent grade through a residential and light industrial region on Michigan City's east side. Before arrival at company's headquarters, the rails cross—and interchange with—the single track of the former Nickel Plate (now Norfolk Southern) branch, which angles southeast.

A two-car westbound train takes a "V" shape as it crosses Louisville & Nashville and Amtrak trackage at 10th and Huron.

A pair of Sumitomo cars negotiate the tight "S" curve between 10th and 11th sts. at Tennessee St. on March 5, 1983. Shortly after their passing, a Detroit-bound Amtrak train rolls over the South Shore crossing just west of the curve.

Mike Schafer

Don Ellison

The usually quiet corner of 11th and Franklin sts. hums with activity as an eastbound evening train pauses at Michigan City in February 1981. A station attendant relaxes next to the station's front window; the South Shore Line herald was badly faded in February 1972.

Tom Post

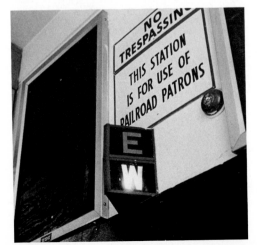

Above: By March 1983, there wasn't much activity in the Michigan City waiting room, even at train time. Right: Brakeman D. H. Spencer assists riders boarding and disembarking on 11th St. Left: As it has for more than 50 years, a gong and visual annunciator indicate the approach and direction of an incoming train.

Framed in one of the front windows at Michigan City depot, South Bend-Chicago train 10 arrives to pick up its covey of passengers on March 7, 1983.

A motorist has this view of a looming South Shore train just east of the Michigan City station. Right: A long westbound train winds through the reverse curve at 11th and Lafayette sts.

American automobiles and Japanese railroad cars mix it up on 11th st. at Oak.

Above: Train 364 fights the snow on Jan. 14, 1978 at 11th and Cedar sts. Below: Six months later, a pair of Pullman cars has an easier time of it at the same location.

The slow moving cars of train 117 aren't much of a threat to neighborhood kids as they approach Shops on a June afternoon in 1984. The diamond in the foreground marks the South Shore's crossing of Norfolk Southern (ex-Nickel Plate).

Little Joe 803, cars 36 and 14, and Geeps 1508 and 1506 inside the New Shop on a warm June 1979 day.

Sign outside the New Shop, Michigan City.

5

Shops: genius department

South Shore's headquarters and center of operations—simply called Shops—is 1.5 miles east of the main station, at the intersection of N. Carroll Ave. and Holliday St. on Michigan City's east side. Not only is this the site of the railroad's principal repair shops, service facility and car storage center, but also the location of management offices. Of the approximately 275 employees, virtually all live in the greater Michigan City-LaPorte area of northern Indiana. Regardless of where they might be stationed along the railroad during a given work day, nearly all first report to The Shops.

The success and survival of the South Shore is due in no small measure to the effectiveness of the railroad's management in adapting it to the changing transportation environment, and to the great dedication of its employees. Not only has the railroad's infrastructure remained a model of quality construction and high maintenance standards, Shops employees have been responsible for some remarkable rolling stock construction and refurbishment programs that would be a credit to any major car or locomotive manufacturer. For example, through the 1940's Michigan City shop crews car-

ried out a major program of passenger car reconstruction and modernization, including stretching some of the original 60-61-foot-long cars by 17 feet, 6 inches to increase capacity. In 1949, Shops crews rewired the famous 800-series "Little Joe" locomotives from their original 3,300-volt d.c. status to the 1,500-volt d.c. of the South Shore. In the mid 1950's they also rebuilt and rewired the ex-New York Central Class R-2 700-series locomotives. Of even more heroic proportions have been efforts of Shops personnel during the past decade to keep the 50-year-old m.u. cars rolling during some of the most severe Midwest winters ever experienced.

The Shops complex is laid out north and south of the railroad's main line. Both the single-story general office building, located south of the tracks, and what today is called the "Old Shop" just opposite it to the north, are original Lake Shore facilities dating to 1908. While the office building still sees the same use, the Old Shop building has served a variety of functions through the years. Originally, it was the Lake Shore's prime shop facility, where all major repair, construction and maintenance of the wood m.u. fleet took place. With the construction of the larger "New Shop" in 1931, the Old

Shop was relegated to car inspection, storehouse, running repairs and a paint facility. Most recently the Old Shop has been used exclusively for freight-car repair, with all inspection and running repairs being done in the New Shop.

Although over 50 years old, the main repair and servicing facility today still is called New Shop. Built as part of the Insull modernization program, it was one of the most modern, fully equipped facilities ever constructed by an interurban. In fact, New Shop occasionally did heavy repair work for other railroad properties.

Despite its age, New Shop still is an impressive yellow brick building. The 50,000-square-foot shop building is served by six tracks, three of which have repair pits. In addition, there are machine, wheel-repair, air-brake and electrical shops and a storeroom. One electrical shop is subdivided into two air conditioned "clean rooms" located on the shop's balcony: one for d.c. board electronics and the other for work on small components. The other electrical room on the shop floor level is reserved for work with heavier equipment (propulsion, air conditioning, motor alternators, etc.). M.u. cars and diesel locomotives both receive major inspections and servicing in the New Shop.

In conjunction with acquisition of new passenger cars, the New Shop has been refurbished. Not only has the building been extended 66 feet to the east, it also has been extended to the north for parts storage. In addition, an inline wheel truing machine (track 5) and drop table (track 6) have been added.

As part of the refurbishment of car maintenance facilities at Shops, the former seven-track coach yard north of the Old Shop has been turned into a material yard. M.u. car storage is now on three tracks north of the main line and east of the Old Shop. Commensurate with the railroad's switch to diesel freight motive power, in 1978 it installed a diesel fuel storage facility just east of the Roeske Ave. bridge. Locomotives and cabooses are stored on extensions of the two tracks that serve this fuel depot. A new carwash building has been built between the locomotive and coach yard tracks. It will be capable of washing up to a six-car train moving eastward.

There are a series of steel buildings located west and north of the Old Shop where the various maintenance-of-way vehicles, track machines and supplies are stored. The small enclosed passenger waiting room located just west and directly opposite the trainmen's locker room in the Old Shop was replaced in June 1984 by a glass enclosed shelter with new platform on the south side of the main line.

South Shore management is divided into five separate departments, each with its own superintendent responsible directly to the general manager. They are: (1) the director of freight sales and service, (2) the mechanical department, (3) the department of engineering *or* ways and structures, (4) the department of transportation and casualty prevention, and (5) the department of passenger and administrative services.

Workers in the mechanical department fall under one of three major classifications: (1) carmen, (2) electricians, and (3) machinists. In addition, there is a separate classification of terminal carmen, who also are under the aegis of this department. Terminal carmen are stationed at Randolph St., Gary and Michigan City. They are responsible for all aspects of car movement, switching and minor repairs at these terminal points.

The department of engineering or ways and structures is concerned with all aspects of the railroad that do not move. Not only are track and signal forces in this department, but so are the linemen responsible for the maintenance of the electrical overhead and its supports. Another section of the engineering staff, build-

Continued on page 66

Two-car train 408 stands in the cold winter sun next to the Old Shop building at Michigan City prior to boarding westbound passengers in March 1983.

As more and more new cars entered service, lines of old cars filled the Michigan City storage yard, March 1983.

Car 4 basks in the midday springtime sun outside the Old Shop (left). Elevator service in the form of a portable lift (above) raises electricians Joe Reed and Bob Sobkowiak to the roof of one of the old cars for pantograph work in the New Shop during March 1982. Listening for instructions, a South Shore carman (right) notches up the controller as his unseen partner beneath the car inspects for faulty contactors. (Below) A sign that's not at all hard to believe when one considers the amount of individual and team effort expended by shop forces to keep the old car fleet rolling through several horrendous winters.

Removing a traction motor is a coordinated effort. Carmen Larry Wanke and Bob Krassow, above left, remove the chocks securing the motor to the truck of combo 102. The caps holding the traction motor to the axle, above right, are removed next. Below

left, Wanke and Dom Albano lift the motor from the No. 1 truck as a fourth car man moves in (below right) with a fork lift to remove the disabled motor.

ings and bridges (B&B), is responsible for these important structures. Mechanics in the B&B section also are responsible for the maintenance of trucks and various heavy track machinery the railroad owns and operates (tampers, ballast regulators, etc.). In the past, South Shore line car 1100 (Ex-Indiana Railroad RPO car 376) was called out when catenary maintenance was needed. However, because operation of the line car required a four-man train crew, in recent years South Shore has used two tower truck-Hyrail units for most overhead service. The 1100 has remained locked up in the Old Shop, and used for heavier catenary work such as contact wire renewal.

The department of transportation and casualty prevention governs train operation. The superintendent is aided by an assistant superintendent, a road foreman of engines and a trainmaster. Among the range of employees included in this department are the engineers, conductors, trainmen, ticket and freight agents. In addition, all freight yard clerks and attendants who clean the stations are members of this unit.

The dispatching office is a central function of the transportation department. Working in the main office building, the dispatcher maintains contact with all units (rail and road vehicles) by means of a radio system. The South Shore was a pioneer in the use of system-wide radio, installing such a network in June 1949. It has since upgraded its radio system and now has one comparable to that found on most other railroads.

Train dispatching is by both timetable and train orders. Passenger trains normally are governed by timetable (except in the case of passenger extras), whereas freights are run as extras and hence governed by train order. In addition to controlling train movements, the dispatcher can control power distribution in the electrical system.

The director of passenger and administrative services oversees the passenger accounting work as well as purchases and stores. He also is involved in negotiations with public agencies, such as NICTD and the RTA, which supply the South Shore with passenger operating subsidies. He also is in charge of labor relations on the railroad as well as being the railroad's principal public relations representative.

Gleaming in the just-past-dawn August sunlight, the remaining RTA trainset contrasts sharply with the South Shore's own.

Motorman stools and portable headlights, soon to be just memories of the past, were classic South Shore symbols for over 50 years. Michigan City shops, March 1982.

South Shore dispatcher Gerry Parrish converses briefly with an engineer from his command post in the Michigan City main office building.

Take away the air conditioners and roof-top modifications and the main office building at Michigan City hasn't changed all that much since 1908.

67

Overhead view in the New Shop building during the summer of 1979. GP7's 1506, 1508 and car 14 dominate in this photo.

Car 22 waits for departure from Shops in July 1982.

Don Ellison

Line car 1100 at work in Hammond during the summer of 1982.

Lou Gerard

Something new, something old, something borrowed (and mostly blue).

Lou Gerard

GP38-2 2003 at rest in the Old Shop on a cold evening during March 1983.

Blue-and-yellow Geeps occupy the fuel and sanding facility at Michigan City between assignments in March 1982.

New cars, old wheelsets. Michigan City, March 1983.

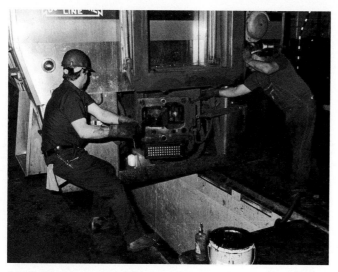

South Shore carmen adjust car 26's coupler.

In a classic interurban pose, car 28 brakes to a halt at Hudson Lake as the conductor prepares to swing down to the gravel platform to assist two boarding passengers.

Tom Post

6 Interurban time machine

The easternmost third of the South Shore line is the longest, extending 30.4 miles from Michigan City Shops to Bendix on the west side of South Bend. The most sparsely populated and least patronized, this picturesque region is the most reminiscent of the rural interurban of the 1920's. The sight of an electric railway coach rolling on single track through the countryside evokes the past. The Michigan City-South Bend section of the South Shore is truly an interurban time machine.

This section of the railroad is single track for its entire length, with only a handful of sidings remaining (Davis stub siding just east of Michigan City and double-ended sidings at Birchim, Olive and Bendix), but none is of the high-speed type found west of Michigan City. Because of the relative infrequency and predominantly passenger nature of the traffic, rail in this eastern sector is lighter (100 lb.) than that in the west (112-115 lb.) and is jointed rather than welded. Single wooden poles with brackets or mast arms support the catenary. Power is distributed by four substations: Eastport at Shops, Tee

Lake, New Carlisle and Grandview just west of Bendix terminal.

Beginning at Shops, the single-track main crosses Trail Creek and then dives under the Chessie (former Pere Marquette) main line, passing the interchange track with the parent company. The South Shore track then curves northeast past a Michigan City municipal golf course at the site of the former Cook stop. After passing under State Rd. 212 and Davis siding, the rails turn straight east at Meer Rd., beginning what is the longest section of tangent track (11.3 miles) on the railroad.

Through Springfield Township (Springville), the countryside shows some undulation with grades as steep as 0.7 percent, but these are mild compared with hilly terrain farther east. East of the former Andry stop the rails climb a 1.98 percent grade up an embankment that takes them over a C&O branch and Highway 39. Following a 1.56 percent descent back to ground level, the rails pass Lalumiere (named for Lalumiere Private School) at Wilhelm Rd. grade crossing. From Lalumiere

to Birchim (5.2 miles) the track climbs a long hill through glaciated, rolling terrain. The ascent is made in a series of steps with grades ranging from 0.5 to 1.5 percent. Galena Hill just east of the former Smith stop is the steepest climb. In the days of electrified freight, a portable substation was maintained on a stub track at the east end of Birchim siding to provide an additional power boost as trains came up the long grade. Conversely, westbound passenger trains have been clocked at better than 85 mph sprinting down the hill.

Beyond Birchim, the gradient flattens out and even heads downhill slightly. Just west of Sagunay stop the track reaches the end of its 11½-mile tangent and makes a sweeping curve southeast only to turn back east at the former Hicks stop at the west end of Hudson Lake. In this scenic setting, the rails are on a fill and run along the southern margin of the lake before ducking into the woods west of the former Lake Park station. Hudson Lake is a favorite recreation area in northern Indiana, catering to boaters and fishermen in the summer and ice fishermen and skiers in the winter. Scattered around the lake are vacation cottages and summer homes.

After passing the Hudson Lake shelter at the eastern end of the lake, South Shore track crosses County Line Rd., which marks the boundary between La Porte and St. Joseph counties, and enters the attractive farming community of New Carlisle. It is here that the former New York Central (now Conrail) main line comes up from La Porte and parallels the South Shore track the rest of the way to South Bend. Until recently there was a major siding at New Carlisle, but it was removed a couple years ago, reflecting the general reduction in traffic in this eastern sector.

From New Carlisle the line heads east-southeast through open farmland. The only marked deviations from the tangents that characterize most of the line are the reverse curves around Lakes Soil Service at Terre Coupee and through the village of Lydick 4.7 miles west of Bendix. Olive siding just east of Terre Coupee is still an interchange point with Conrail and South Shore, and also serves the Carborundum Co. there.

As the rails approach the west side of South Bend the surroundings change from agricultural to industrial. The South Shore has another interchange with Conrail near Bendix, and it still does freight business with a few of the small industries in the area.

The single-story, buff blue-and-white station in South Bend was erected in the spring of 1970 and serves as a joint South Shore and Amtrak facility. It has a waiting room, ticket office, facilities for trainmen and a freight agent's office. Prior to its construction, South Shore reached its former terminal in downtown South Bend via 2.2 miles of street running. The route headed straight east from Bendix Dr. down Orange St. for nine blocks to Birdsell St. There the tracks angled one block south to Colfax Ave., which they then took for another three blocks east as far as Elm before angling northeast to La Salle. Trains ran east on La Salle to the railroad's storefront depot at the intersection of Michigan and La Salle. East of the station across the St. Joseph River was a five-track coach yard where cars were kept overnight.

Today, equipment is stored overnight in Michigan City. All passenger equipment for South Bend service is deadheaded as passenger extras to and from Shops (though not indicated in timetables, these deadhead moves will carry passengers). These procedures eliminate the necessity of maintaining carmen to switch and service the equipment for the very few trains. It also reduces vandalism associated with car storage in an urban area.

In the early morning mist of Aug. 14, 1982, a two-car train 462 approaches the Shops en route to Chicago from South Bend.

Equipment returns from South Bend's Bendix station for use in other trains or for overnight storage. Here Extra 25 West, with white classification lights illuminated, is about to pass under the C&O just east of the Shops. The car will then depart Michigan City as train 286, the last westbound of the day at 8:10 p.m.

South Bend train 459 speeds beneath the Highway 212 overpass just east of the former Cook stop at Royal Road, near the outskirts of Michigan City, as winter lingers into spring on a late March day in 1982.

The rural calm is shattered as a South Shore train races across the Highway 300 overpass east of Smith, Ind., on a pleasant June day.

South Bend-Chicago train 376 heads down the 1.5 percent grade of Galena Hill at high speed, just east of the former Smith stop and the Chiddick Road overpass.

It's June 17, 1979, and the last South Bend train of the weekend (left) has started to climb the last leg of the five-mile hill between Lalumiere and Birchim. Below, train 468 rumbles over the short Lake Park Road bridge west of Hudson Lake on June 24, 1979.

Train 463 creates its own blizzard (above) as it blasts through Terre Coupee at better than 80 mph in January 1978; in a different season, train 469 (right) is the center of a Midwestern portrait as it flashes past the silos of Lakes Farm Service in Terre Coupee. (Above right) The swampy area in the foreground is that part of Hudson Lake cut off from the main body of water when the South Shore's fill was built. The fill supports Chicago-bound train 468 on Aug. 14, 1982.

New equipment protects the South Bend schedule of train 305, speeding past the boathouse at the east end of Hudson Lake on March 6, 1983.

Hardy fishermen illustrate the year-round popularity of Hudson Lake as a recreational spot on a gray January afternoon in 1972.   *Mike Schafer*

A one-car train is reflected in the cold, blue waters of Hudson Lake in April 1977.

Phil Borleske

Train 459 races past the New Carlisle substation; car 109 brakes to pick up a lone passenger at the New Carlisle station in June 1979.

South Shore train 484 is five miles from its South Bend origin as it disturbs the quiet of Lydick, Ind., on Aug. 15, 1982. (Right) The sun sets on America's last interurban, at Lydick, on an August evening in 1982.

The two cars of train 312 negotiate the west switch of Birchim siding, just after ducking under the Indiana Tollway. The train is on the downhill portion of the five-mile hill shown on page 78.

Business is brisk at the corner of La Salle and Michigan in downtown South Bend this day in 1969, as two cars prepare for the dash to Chicago.

Mike Schafer

Long before Federal Express and its many imitators, South Shore offered "absolutely, positively" same day—not overnight—express service (right). The engineer is giving the porter a hand at South Bend, as flowers and other items from Chicago are unloaded. (Below) Down the hill from the South Bend passenger station and across the St. Joseph River, South Shore maintained a compact yard. Emerging from the yard, car 106 heads back to the station to receive passengers for the run to Chicago.

Ready to roll back to the Michigan City Shops as Passenger Extra 1 West, a two-car train sits in South Bend's Bendix station the evening of March 4, 1983.

The new fleet stands at attention at the Michigan City Shops on March 6, 1983. Within a few months, all schedules will be protected by the Nippon Sharyo cars and the old equipment will retire after decades of faithful service.

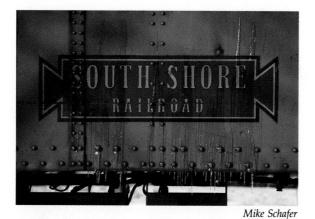

Mike Schafer

7

From Pullman to Sumitomo

Over the past thirty years the most significant change in passenger services on the South Shore has been the gradual but inexorable shift from long-distance, intercity-type services to short-distance, commuter-type operations. One need only compare timetables over a twenty-year span to see the marked reduction in the number of trains between Michigan City and South Bend relative to the number retained between Chicago and Gary, today's heavy commuter district. In 1984, there were five times as many trains serving the Chicago-Gary segment than the Michigan City-South Bend end, whereas the 1963 ratio was only 2.2 to 1. Part of that difference reflects marked reductions in the total number of trains operated, but the principal difference is a result of significant reductions in service to South Bend.

One specific marker of this shift in the type of passenger services offered is the contrast between the range of car types and accommodations offered by the Insull fleet purchased in the late 1920's and that of the new equipment acquired by the railroad in 1983. Whereas the rolling stock of the 1920's included baggage combines, varied types of coaches, diners and parlor-observation cars, reflecting the variety of travel functions carried out by an intercity system of that era, the newest equipment consists of only one type of coach configuration designed strictly for commuters. Hence in the same way that today's one-function commuter coach would

have been inappropriate to the range of services offered by the railroad 50 years ago, in its last decade of service the Insull-era fleet seemed equally maladapted to the principally commuter-oriented service the road renders today. For example, following cancellation of less-than-carload package freight services in the mid 1970's the railroad's baggage combines (cars 100-111) still showed up in train consists—sometimes as many as three together! In a fleet that had deteriorated progressively through too many years of operation, the emphasis was on equipment availability and operability rather than its original function.

When South Shore commuters boarded the Insull units, it was always with a sense of adventure as to what kind of interior and seating accommodations they would find. And what the riders may have gained in service reliability and comfort with the new cars they have lost in a sense of anticipation and novelty when boarding a train. How did such a great diversity of interior appointments in the older South Shore cars come about?

Prior to the acquisition of new equipment in 1982-83, the last time such a fleet of new cars was purchased for the South Shore was over half a century earlier as part of Samuel Insull's modernization program of 1926-29. That brand-new fleet of all-steel 1500-volt d.c. cars was ordered to completely replace the 6600-volt a.c. wood cars of the predecessor Lake Shore company. The order

was placed in three stages. The first consisted of 29 cars built by the Pullman Co. and delivered in 1926 and 1927: 15 double-end coaches (Nos. 1-15) and ten double-ended baggage-coach combinations (Nos. 100-109) as well as diners (301 and 302) and parlors (351 and 352).

Except for diners and parlors, as originally delivered, all were motorized 60-foot (over buffers) units. Coaches 1-10 seated 56 in two compartments with a transverse bulkhead separating a 16-seat smoking section from a 40-seat non-smoking section. By contrast, coaches 11-15 had an enclosed, laterally placed "Pullman-type" smoking compartment equipped with two, broad sofa-type seats for eight which was approached from a side aisle. As a result of this more luxurious, semi-private accommodation, seating capacity in these cars was only 48 versus 56 in the other coaches. The combines seated 44 and like coaches 1-10 had a more conventional subdivision into a 16-seat smoking section and a 28-seat main compartment. All of the cars of the 1926 Pullman order were equipped with walkover-type seats upholstered in either green plush or pantasote. Interestingly, through the years, shop crews developed their own descriptive nicknames for differing interior configurations. For example, cars 1-10 that were simply divided into two compartments were called "straight aisles" whereas coaches 11-15 with the Pullman smoking compartment were called "box smokers." Combines were

The snow impacted in the air horns of car 17 will be forced out with the next pull on the horn cord.

referred to simply as "baggage cars."

A second order of 10 double-end motorized coaches (Nos. 16-25) and 10 double-end control trailers (Nos. 201-210) was placed with Pullman and delivered in 1927. These units were all "box smokers" and seated 48 but were slightly longer (61 feet over buffers) and featured more luxuriant rotating, bucket-type seats upholstered in "Byzantine plush" fabric. However, the most notable additions to the fleet that year were two trailer dining cars, Nos. 301 and 302, and two trailer parlor-solarium observation cars, Nos. 351 and 352, all built by Pullman. Both of these luxury car types differed from the conventional coaches in their greater overall length (64'-1") and the fact they rode on a pair of six-wheeled Commonwealth trucks—the only interurban cars in regular service to do so.

A final order of 15 motorized double-end coaches (Nos. 10, 26-39), three more trailers (Nos. 211-213) and an additional pair of parlor-observation trailers (Nos. 353 and 354) was given to the Standard Car Co. of Hammond, Ind., with delivery in 1929. The motors and trailers were both 61-foot cars, "box smokers" and virtually identical to those built by Pullman in 1927. The parlor cars differed from the Pullman models as they were shorter (61 feet), rode on 4-wheel trucks and lacked kitchen facilities.

The range of types of interior configurations would be expanded markedly by the railroad's own rebuilding and modernization programs of the 1940's and 1950's. Through the depression years there were no significant alterations to the original interior appointments; the most significant change in the new car fleet was the dropping of diner and parlor car services in 1932, economies necessitated by marked declines in patronage during the Depression. The two diners were scrapped in 1941, whereas the two original parlor cars were converted to control trailers and eventually sold in 1945 to Canada Gulf Terminal and MBA Construction Co., respectively. The newest parlor cars (Nos. 353 and 354) found a kinder fate, having also been rebuilt into control trailers in 1938 and 1939.

Despite the lean years of the Depression as well as the rigors of bankruptcy, the South Shore managed to survive intact. During World War II it experienced the highest levels of ridership in its entire history, and as a result the capacity of its rolling stock was taxed to the limit. Since the railroad was unable to acquire suitable new cars during the war, it decided to increase the capacity of the existing fleet. Starting with car 15 in 1942, Shops began a program of cutting some of the original 60- and 61-foot cars in half, intercalating a 17'-6" section between the original ends and strengthening the underframes. Such a stretching increased the overall length of the 1926 Pullmans to 77'-6" and the 1927 Pullman and 1929 Standard cars to an overall length of 78'-6". At the same time, those box smokers that were stretched were converted to straight-aisle configurations. The increase in length boosted seating capacity from 48 and 56 to 80 in the case of the full coaches (motors and trailers) and from 44 to 64 or 68 in the case of the baggage cars. Such increases in passenger capacity reduced not only costs per passenger mile but also maintenance costs.

At the same time the cars received this major structural change, many had their interiors modernized. Modern, foam-padded, tubular framed, rotating seats were installed and the original globe ceiling lights replaced by an attractive tubular fluorescent fixture down the center of the ceiling. Similarly, new bulkhead partitions were installed between smoking and non-smoking sections in the baggage cars, toilets were moved to the ends of the cars and the ceiling line significantly altered with more attractive, anodized aluminum luggage racks that gave the cars an interior look as modern and streamlined as that of many contemporary steam-road passenger coaches.

Following the stretching and interior modernization program of the 1940's, selected cars were further modernized by the installation of air-conditioning and large, rubber-sealed picture windows.

The remainder of the cars stayed in their original "short motor" (60-61 foot) configuration but exhibited a real potpourri of interior furnishings. For example, while several units retained their original walkover or bucket seats upholstered in newer fabric, selected cars were outfitted with newer, tubular-frame seating and/or modern luggage racks. Hence, the slow and piecemeal nature of South Shore's car refurbishment program contributed further to the great variety of accommodations exhibited by the Insull-era fleet in its last years of service.

The most divergent accommodation in the fleet was an experiment to boost seating capacity in "straight aisle" car No. 1 and former "box smoker" No. 36 (which was converted to a straight-aisle unit with modernized ceiling line and lighting after an accident in September 1960). In November 1969, both of these "short motors" were fitted with 3-and-2 passenger walkover seats giv-

Cab controls of car 37 (left) show the type XM master controller on the left side of the cab and the M23 brake valve to its right. In the new cars (right), the positions of the master controller and brake valve are similar, but the number of gauges has increased significantly.

ing them a total seating of 64 and 68 respectively, in contrast to their original 56- and 48-seat capacities. Because of their ample overall width (10 feet, 1 inch) they could accommodate such wider seating without undue constriction to the center aisle. Obviously this type of maximum capacity arrangement was a hint of the kind of shorter-distance, commuter-type accommodation that would be the mode of the future.

In both original and modernized cars, seats were rotated at each terminal so most passengers could face in the direction of car travel. But with the need to cut costs in the 1970's, seats were permanently bolted in place with half facing east and half facing west to eliminate the need for a carman or cleaner to rotate seats at the ends of the line.

Following the period of intensive car rebuilding and modernization in the forties and fifties, the South Shore heavyweights continued to do yeoman service year in and year out, good weather and bad. Through their extraordinary skills the Michigan City shop crews managed to double the life expectancy of the cars and at the same time adapt them to modern transportation needs. However, in the 1970's, as the fleet approached its golden anniversary, it became clear Michigan City Shops' life-sustaining abilities had come back to haunt them. What at one time seemed like an economical move in car renovation ultimately became a service liability as the cars began to experience an increasing number of breakdowns. In fact, some employees felt South Shore should have used revenues from World War II ridership peaks to purchase a new fleet of cars rather than stretch the service life of the original cars beyond their intended time.

A series of brutal, snowy winters from 1976 through 1982 virtually brought the old fleet to its knees. The main problems were the result of blowing snow getting into the self-ventilated motors and freezing or shorting them out. With increased age much of the insulation on the circuitry had deteriorated, permitting 1500-line voltage to get into the 32-volt d.c. control circuits and short out the cars. In the final years, cars of the Insull fleet were prone to an increasing number of breakdowns which not only wreaked havoc with the passenger schedules but demanded increasing time on the part of shop crews. Small wonder there was little or no time or money to keep the car's interiors and exteriors painted and clean as they had in the past. As the fleet trundled on in the late 1970's, the cars came to look increasingly down at the heels and generally less appealing to the riding public.

On top of electrical problems, the more than 50 years of service under severe weather extremes had taken its toll on the cars' basic structural integrity. In a detailed analysis done by the engineering firm of Louis T. Klauder & Associates of Philadelphia in 1975, it was found that corrosion had reduced side sheet strength to 50 percent of its original design. On some cars, side sheets themselves were estimated to be only 60 percent of the thickness of the original and at the point where the side frames joined the collision post, shear strength was only 40 percent of the original. Clearly there were questions of car safety that went beyond matters of their operational status.

The other side of the passenger car dilemma in the 1970's was the problem of availability of spare parts needed to keep the fleet in service—many were no longer available on the market and had to be manufactured specially at a very high cost. In the last years of the cars' service, Shops solved these problems either by producing its own spare parts or by cannibalizing selected cars that had been taken out of service. Anyone who visited Shops in the 1970's was struck by the image of partially dismantled m.u. cars on the northernmost track (12) in the coach yard which served as a spare parts reservoir. At one time or another everything from motors, motor generators, switch groups, draft gear, steps, drawbars, diaphragms and seats were removed from these units.

The breakdown of South Shore m.u. cars reached crisis proportions during the winter of 1981-82. At the low point only about 12 cars were available to cover the schedules, and to plug the gap, South Shore leased two, five-car bilevel, diesel push-pull trainsets from the Illinois Regional Transportation Authority. These former Rock Island commuter trainsets, each with a seating capacity of 775, were arranged with their F40PH diesels at the east end of each train, pushing westbound and pulling eastbound. When initiated into service on Jan. 25 and Feb. 2, 1982, respectively, schedules and operating procedures with these trains had to be altered significantly. For example, since they could not be loaded at high-level platforms, all stops between Randolph St. and Hegewisch had to be omitted. Furthermore, schedules had to be extended because of the slower acceleration of the diesels and also because of a 10 mph speed restriction under bridges crossing the ICG— There was concern that bilevel roofs might strike the catenary under such low clearances if these trains were running (and bouncing) at speed. Each diesel trainset

was operated on one morning westbound and one evening eastbound schedule through the period of greatest winter problems. One trainset was returned April 23, 1982, but the second was retained until March 4, 1983, when the new m.u. cars were finally put into regular revenue service.

Long before these final equipment problems had developed, it was obvious that if the South Shore were going to survive as a passenger carrier, it would need a fleet of new cars. Regardless of the mechanical magic the shop crews had been able to weave all these years, the equipment's time had obviously run out.

In the early 1970's there had been an aborted effort to obtain an Urban Mass Transportation Administration (UMTA) grant to help purchase a new car fleet. Unfortunately, with bureaucratic complications arising from the two-state, five-county region as well as the fiscal conservatism of the state of Indiana, matching funds from the states failed to materialize and South Shore was forced to continue with its deteriorating fleet.

The threat of complete abandonment of all passenger services by the railroad in late 1976 finally galvanized the state of Indiana into action that ultimately would save the service. With enabling legislation from the Indiana General Assembly, the four-county Northern Indiana Commuter Transportation District (NICTD) was formed in June 1977. It subsequently would serve as a funnel for funds (both state and federal) for the railroad for both operating subsidies and capital improvements.

With a final agreement by the four counties to supply their share of a capital improvement grant, NICTD quickly set about to replace the aging m.u. fleet. The specifications developed by its equipment consultant, Louis T. Klauder & Associates, were put out to bid in 1979. Only two bids were received, in August 1980, and Sumitomo Corporation of America underbid the Budd Co. by some four million dollars for 35 motor cars and eight trailers. Ultimately the order would be revised to 36 motor cars with an option to buy eight more motors instead of trailers.

Initially bilevel m.u. units similar to ICG Highliner cars were considered, and as early as July 1975, developments had proceeded to the point of having a pair of Highliners make a run over the length of the South Shore to test clearances. Bombardier of Canada, which had completed ICG's order of 36 remaining units, had even made a proposal for a double-ended version of the Highliner called the "Shoreliner." Nonetheless, in

making up the specifications for bidding, NICTD decided that bilevel cars were not really suited to the South Shore's type of service. Furthermore, when Bombardier found out that design modifications would be great and that certain of NICTD's contract clauses were unacceptable, they decided not to bid at all.

While Sumitomo Corporation was the low bidder for the order, Nippon Sharyo Seizo Kaisha Ltd. (Japan Rolling-Stock Manufacturing Company Ltd.) was actually responsible for the building of the carbody and trucks with Sumitomo serving simply as the broker for the deal. Because of a "Buy American" clause tied to any federal grant, 51 percent of the cars' equipment and labor was required to be American. Thus motors and control equipment were to be made by General Electric, brakes by New York Air Brake, etc. Except for prototype test car No. 1 which was totally equipped and assembled in Japan, all subsequent members of the new fleet were shipped to the U.S. as carbody shells with trucks and assembled stateside. Initially G.E.'s plant in Hornell, N.Y., was to be the final assembly site but Sumitomo was unhappy with the quality of workmanship there and G.E.'s Cleveland plant was chosen instead.

In selecting a car design, NICTD and South Shore were not interested in making great leaps in technological innovation. They wanted a very basic type of car that would employ the standard technology of the times with equipment that could be replaced easily and would be easy to maintain.

The new cars differ most significantly from the old in their external appearance. Having been based on the proven Silverliner/Jersey Arrow design, they naturally bear more resemblance to mainline railroad electrified commuter equipment than to interurban tradition. Despite their fluted stainless-steel exterior, the alternating maroon-and-orange stripes at window level as well as the traditional South Shore logo beneath the engineer's cab provide a link with the line's interurban past.

Dimensionally the new cars are longer (85 feet versus 78 feet, 6 inches), wider (10 feet, 6 inches versus 10 feet 1 inch) and seat more (93 versus 80) but with a lighter overall weight (59.1 tons versus 76.6 tons for standard coaches Nos. 26-28). The new cars also have three rather than two sets of doors for loading and unloading; one pair of doors at each vestibule end with steps for both high and low platform loading and a pair of center doors without steps, for rapid loading at stations with high platforms. All doors are electrically operated and

The interior of car 104 shows the car divided into smoking and non-smoking sections. The seats are permanently fixed, but originally were able to rotate to face direction of travel.

CSS&SB car 1 shows its unique 3-and-2 seating arrangement.

The original bucket-seat interior of car 40 looks a bit worn as it rests at the Shops in April 1982.

The baggage section of car 104 has slots for company mail, but in latter years the baggage compartments were used primarily to accommodate overflow passengers on crowded trains.

can be controlled individually or for the entire train from a single vestibule control panel. An additional new feature is a trainlined loudspeaker system that can be operated from any vestibule or from a control panel adjacent to the center doors. All cars are air conditioned.

Like the older cars in their final years of service, the 46 pairs of seats are permanently fixed with half facing forward and half facing backward. The new cars also have a "priority seating area," a single and a double seat facing each other that have flip-up seat cushions to accommodate a wheelchair. Instead of a pair of toilets as in the older cars, a single toilet facility serves at the center of the car. The toilet has a sliding door and is large enough for a wheelchair. The aluminum luggage racks serve as at least one reminder of the car's interurban service. The cars also differ from their predecessors in having transit-type couplers which automatically make all air and electrical connections without having to use jumper cables as with the old fleet. This also permits limited operation with ICG Highliners under emergency conditions.

In addition to the marked differences in passenger accommodations and appointments, there are also differences in the electrical propulsion, control and braking equipment. The 1500 d.c. current is collected by two, single-arm, Faively-type pantographs instead of the diamond-shaped pans used on the older cars. The current collected supplies each of the four truck-mounted G.E. 1258B1 d.c., series-wound 160-h.p. traction motors. In contrast to the older cars, each motor on the new cars is ventilated by a positive-pressure air system which keeps snow and moisture from entering the motors and causing the kind of shortouts that plagued the Insull-era cars in their last years of service.

Whereas the older fleet was equipped with motor generators that fed batteries for a source of 32-volt d.c. control current, the new cars have motor alternators which give 230 volts three-phase a.c. used to operate many of the electrical devices on the car. Additionally, 115-volt single-phase a.c. and 75-volt d.c. control power is provided. Furthermore, in contrast to the HBF (Hand Battery Field Tap) manual control system of the older units, the new cars are equipped with G.E. "CM" (Cam Magnetic) camshaft control with automatic acceleration. For example, whereas engineers operating the old cars controlled acceleration by manually "notching up" the master controller handle through a series of resistance points that progressively cut out resistances and also manually transitioned the motors from series to parallel circuit configurations, the master controller on the new cars has only six positions which automatically take care of these functions (Off; C = coast—no power to motors; SW = switching—for speeds up to 15 mph but all resistances are still in the circuit; SER = series—for speeds up to 45 mph; PAR = parallel—speeds up to 60 mph; FS = field shunt or short field—speeds up to maximum of 75 mph). All the engineer has to do is rotate the controller handle to the appropriate position for the speed he wants to attain and, like a diesel locomotive, the car (or train) will automatically and smoothly accelerate to that speed.

Braking is also different. In contrast to the Westinghouse AMU automatic air schedule of the older cars, that in the new cars is a New York Air Brake 26-C schedule with blended dynamic-air braking. The system uses dynamic braking down to about 10 mph and all air from 10 mph to zero. Such a dynamic-air, fully blended system ultimately results in less wear on brake shoes and wheels and can be especially economical in start-stop commuter service.

The most subtle difference—but a significant one to the operational life and greater reliability of the new cars—is the nature of the insulating material used in their wiring. One of the reasons there was so much shorting out of the circuitry of the older cars was that the wiring was insulated with organic material (rubber, etc.) that deteriorated with age. Insulation in the new cars is with modern inorganic materials such as epoxy and mylar that are longer lasting.

The prototype test car (called SCA-1, for Sumitomo Corporation of America because Sumitomo still owned the car during the test period) was shipped from the Nippon Sharyo plant at Toyokawa, Japan, on Dec. 20, 1981, and arrived at the Port of Philadelphia on Jan. 20, 1982. By Jan. 26 it was at Michigan City Shops. Shops crews were pre-occupied with getting the old fleet back into operation after one of the worst winters in the line's history, so testing was delayed, and additional delays occurred from disagreements about insurance coverage while the car was operating on South Shore property. These problems were finally resolved and on March 25, 1982, the SCA-1 was pulled from the New Shop by South Shore GP38-2 2006 and for the first time ran under its own power.

A large contingent of Nippon Sharyo technicians and engineers including the Toyokawa plant manager Tohru Katori established an office at Shops to carry out the testing in conjunction with engineers from Klauder and the respective equipment manufacturers. For the testing program, SCA-1 was outfitted with a bevy of meters and measuring devices to monitor propulsion,

The relative lengths of the original 60-foot cars and the 77-foot lengthened cars is evident in this comparison of train 269 at Burns Harbor on March 29, 1982.

acceleration and braking as well as a range of other functions. Aside from the clearance tests along the length of the route and into Chicago, the majority of running tests were performed out on the South Bend end of the line where the traffic was minimal.

In general, the SCA-1 performed well; however there were some initial problems with motor flashovers and particularly the emergency brake rate. The latter was finally solved by a change in brake shoe composition. Following the successful testing of the car and the required adjustments, the cars started to flow into Michigan City from Japan and Cleveland starting Sept. 3, 1982, at an average of six per month.

On Saturday Oct. 23, 1982, the new passenger rolling stock was officially dedicated at Michigan City Shops with a keynote speech by Indiana Governor Robert Orr. At that time car No. 1 of the new fleet was officially dedicated to the memory of Congressman Adam Benjamin Jr., late of the First Congressional District of Indiana who had been instrumental in gaining support fror the South Shore's renewal at the national level. Following the ceremonies at Michigan City, the four-car inaugural carried guests west for a second dedication ceremony at Hegewisch, Ill.

The first revenue run of the new equipment was as the "morning hotshot" (train 8) on Monday, Nov. 22, 1982. From that point on, as new cars became available for service, they gradually replaced members of the old fleet. Aug. 27, 1983, marked the last weekday that the Insull-era fleet operated in revenue service and Monday, Aug. 30, 1983, marked the first day of full schedule coverage by the new cars. The most visible step in the South Shore's passenger revitalization had finally occurred!

In one of the new cars, Conductor R. Foxy Shires answers a passenger's question as train 25 heads for South Bend.

Little Joe 802 slices the frigid January air as it rolls the Gary Job local westbound toward Clark Road in 1981.

Mike Schafer

Tom Post

8 From Joes to Geeps

This past decade of South Shore operations witnessed significant shifts in the nature of passenger functions, but alterations in freight service were no less marked. Although the development of extensive carload freight business has been a key to the South Shore's survival, for the majority of its life South Shore has had to scramble for much of the freight traffic it developed. CSS&SB was a latecomer on the freight scene in the Calumet region, where major trunk lines (such as Pennsy and NYC) had already bottled up service to the area's heavy industries. South Shore had to scratch for what was left.

In its early years, predecessor Lake Shore was strictly passenger oriented and showed little interest in handling freight, beyond some l.c.l. (less-than-carload) package freight carried in its baggage cars. Not until 1916 did Lake Shore become involved with carload freight in a serious way and acquire the motive power and upgraded physical plant to serve that function. Because the majority of intersecting steam roads would not permit the development of interchanges with the electric line, Lake Shore's potential for freight service was never fully realized and the line ultimately went bankrupt.

With acquisition of the defunct Lake Shore property by Insull interests in 1925, a more aggressive program of freight traffic solicitation was instituted. Not only did Insull implement a great number of interchanges along the route, but because of the vast electrical and power holdings that he commanded, he was able to influence the routing of freight shipments over his own subsidiary rail companies. The result was a significant increase in the variety of freight traffic on the South Shore—to the point that it became a major carload carrier.

Unfortunately this boom, dependent upon the existence of the Insull utilities empire, was relatively short-lived. Once the empire collapsed in the 1930's there was a notable decline in freight revenues, and the South Shore was forced to fend for itself. Fortunately all of the interchanges established during the Insull administration remained intact, and the road set about to actively solicit freight traffic on a wider basis by the establishment of freight sales offices throughout the country. The goal was to obtain as much bridge traffic as possible on the grounds that, since South Shore had an east-west corridor route that intersected many trunk-line railroads, it could move freight more rapidly between trunk lines instead of having it tied up for long periods in Chicago freight yards.

This emphasis on overhead traffic supplied the South Shore with a viable freight business through the post-war period and into the 1960's. However, in the late 1960's and early 1970's it became clear that rising labor and car costs made such bridge traffic increasingly less remunerative. The new era was one of long-haul freight with emphasis on more-effective car utilization. Furthermore, since South Shore had become a subsidiary of Chessie in 1967, it was obvious C&O was not going to let its own property shorthaul it in the territory it served. Thus in the early 1970's South Shore gradually phased out its nationwide freight offices and focused on unit coal and ore traffic to Bethlehem Steel at Burns Harbor and the NIPSCO generating stations at Bailly and Michigan City.

Through the 1970's South Shore freight traffic consisted of unit coal trains plus a Gary switch run six days a week between Gary and Kensington and a switch run to South Bend, dispatched on an average of three days a week. All of the freights operated as extras and, except for the Gary switch job which had its own crew assignment and regular departure time, freight crews were drawn from the general pool or "extra board." With the complete dieselization of South Shore freight services in early 1981, the Gary switch job was abolished and its traffic handled as part of the general freight pool.

To demonstrate the difference in freight patterns of 1984 to those of the 1940's and 1950's, in terms of sheer

The 802 hums through Columbia Ave. curve at Hammond with the Gary Job, preparing to make its entrance to the B&OCT interchange (page 100, bottom) on June 21, 1979.

tonnage, coal outnumbers miscellaneaous freight (a variety of merchandise and heavy material-type goods) by a ratio of approximately 9 to 1. Presently South Shore interchanges miscellaneous freight only with the ICG at Kensington, IHB at Burnham, B&OCT (Chessie) at Hammond, EJ&E at Goff Junction (Gary), B&O at Miller, NS at Shops (Michigan City), C&O at Michigan City and Conrail at South Bend. Furthermore, such freight is almost exclusively for on-line industries and only 2 to 3 percent is bridge traffic.

Operations of the early 1980's call for unit coal trains for the two NIPSCO generating stations to be picked up from the IHB at Burnham and the empties returned to the B&OCT at Hammond. Metallurgical coal destined for Bethlehem Steel is picked up at the B&O at Miller. In addition, occasional unit trains of Western coal are delivered by C&NW at the Hammond interchange of the B&OCT via a trackage rights agreement from C&NW's Proviso Yard in Chicago.

The lightest freight activity is on the South Bend end of the line where the railroad services just a handful of industries (Hedwin Co., General Liquors and Simon Brothers in South Bend, and the Carborundum Corporation in Terre Coupee just east of New Carlisle). Freight traffic is so light on this end of the line that, in contrast with the tri-weekly schedule of earlier, this end of the line is serviced only once a week.

Reflecting these changes in South Shore freight traffic are the changes in its freight motive power, especially after 1970. From the Insull era through World War II, South Shore relied on a fleet of steeple-cab locomotives typical of many interurban properties (Nos. 1001-1014 built by Baldwin-Westinghouse and Baldwin-GE between 1924 and 1931 augmented by four additional steeple-cabs, Nos. 900-903, originally built by Baldwin-Westinghouse in 1929 for the Illinois Central electrification, but sold to the South Shore in 1941.) Despite exceptionally heavy freight traffic during World War II and the immediate postwar period, South Shore managed to make it through with these steeple-cab units. However, it became clear that with the heavier tonnages the road was hauling, more powerful motive power would be necessary; i.e., that characteristic of mainline electrifications rather than an interurban. Originally, the railroad had intended to build such freight power itself and even had some designs on the drawing boards when a fortuitous development in international relations provided a unique opportunity to acquire ready-made heavy motive power.

As part of the government's postwar lend-lease program, the General Electric Co. of Erie, Pa., in March 1946 was contracted by the Russian government to build twenty, 273-ton double-ended 2-D + D-2 electric locomotives for use on one of their mountainous rail lines. The 5-foot-gauge locomotives were to be dual-service road engines operating on 3,300 volts d.c. At the time of their construction, their 5,530 hourly horse-power ratings ranked them among the most powerful single-unit electric locomotives ever built.

As a result of a breakdown of relations between the U.S. and U.S.S.R. during the Cold War, the original order was cancelled in 1948 after eight units had been completed. Despite these problems, GE completed the original order of 20 with the hope of being able to sell them elsewhere. When it became clear GE would have to seek another market for these behemoths, they decided to build the last six units to standard rather than broad gauge of the original Russian order.

The South Shore was one of the two domestic roads (the other was the Milwaukee Road) to show an interest in the Russian motors and in 1949 purchased the last three standard-gauge units at the bargain price of three for the price of one ($270,000). Upon arrival at Michigan City in May 1949, Shops crews rewired the locomotives from 3,300 to 1,500 volts d.c. Painted traction orange with maroon striping and numbered 801-803, they were known simply as the "800's" on the South Shore whereas elsewhere they were called "Little Joes." Regardless of the nicknames applied to them, these famous interurban freight motors turned in a notable 31 years of service before their retirement in February 1981.

Up and over: Joe 802 shoves loads up—and down—the 2.5 percent grades vaulting the Indiana Toll Road on the lead to the Harbison-Walker plant in Hammond, June 19, 1979.

The Gary Job Joe at its namesake station in January 1981 (above) stands in a scene that has since vanished, with the razing of the old Lake Shore depot and construction of elevated right-of-way and the new Gary Transportation Center in 1983-84. (Below) The 802 clatters across the Stanray industrial lead and Chessie main line to make interchange with B&OCT, June 1979.

Another addition to the fleet of heavy electrics in the 1950's enabled South Shore to retire all its remaining steeple-cab locomotives. Dieselization of New York Central's Cleveland terminal electrification in the mid 1950's allowed 2-C + C-2 P2-class electric motors to be transferred to New York City where they replaced Alco-GE C-C R2-class electrics on the 650-volt d.c. New York terminal electrification. South Shore bought ten of the displaced 3,000-h.p. d.c. locomotives in 1955 and rebuilt and rewired them for 1,500-volt d.c. using surplus pantographs, compressors, motor blowers and series-parallel switches from the former Cleveland Union Terminal P motors.

Of the ten R2 units purchased, only seven were rebuilt (Nos. 701-706 between 1955 and 1958 and No. 707 in 1968). Because they were shorter (54 feet vs. 88'-10") and lighter (140 vs. 273 tons) than the 800's, the 700's were able to switch sidings and interchanges that the 800's could not. Thus these two postwar additions to the South Shore's freight motor fleet complemented one another and managed to survive well into the 1970's.

A combination of decreasing availability of spare parts combined with the outmoded nature of the electrical distribution system limited the capacity of the electrics, and ultimately led to their replacement by diesels in the 1970's. During the 1950's the 800's handled coal traffic for NIPSCO's Michigan City generating station and from 1962 on they also served the new power station at Bailly. However, this was before NIPSCO purchased a fleet of 100-ton, flat-bottomed gondolas and with the institution of these high-capacity cars, the 800's were limited to 30 cars or 3,000 tons maximum. It wasn't that the 800's lacked the tractive effort to handle 100-110 car (10,000 ton) unit trains of today, but that their current draw on the outmoded electrical systems was too great to permit them to operate at full capacity.

For a time the railroad tried different combinations of electric motive power to move the heavier unit trains over the road, such as a "push-pull" system with an 800 on the point and either another 800 or a pair of 700's shoving on the rear. Still, they could move only about 4,500 tons and required at least two trips to move the tonnage handled in a single unit train of today. Given the railroad's increasing emphasis on long-haul, unit-train traffic, it was clear that the days of electrified freight on the South Shore were numbered.

For a period in the early 1970's, the more nimble-footed 700's handled most switching chores including the Gary job and work on the South Bend end of the line. The 800's were relegated to various odd jobs and as occasional stand-ins on the Gary switcher. However, when the 700's were removed from service in late 1975 because of difficulties in obtaining wheels for them, the 800's took over the Gary switch run in late 1975 where they remained for the rest of their service life, which ended in January 1981.

Toward the end of their careers, the 800's also suffered from a lack of parts availability. For this reason the 801 was taken out of service in December 1976 and served its remaining years as a spare parts source to keep the other two units running.

During their stint on the Gary job, the 802 and 803 alternated at two-week intervals. While one unit was on the assignment, the other was at Shops for general inspection and servicing. Despite their age and the continuing problems with spare parts, they were very reliable and respected machines.

Dieselization of the South Shore actually began as early as 1955 when the railroad purchased an EMD SW1 switcher from the Buffalo Creek Railway of Buffalo, N.Y., to help haul construction trains on the East Chicago bypass. Later, the significant impetuses for dieselization were the aforementioned restrictions of moving heavy unit trains with the electrics and the fact the new Bethlehem Steel Plant in Burns Harbor would not permit catenary to be strung into its plant. To resolve these problems and service these industries, South Shore obtained from parent Chessie one TR3A, three TR3B's (EMD cow-and-calf switchers), and two NW2's in 1969. In 1971 these locomotives were traded in on five ex-C&O GP7's and later joined by three additional Geeps. Numbered 1501-1508, these GP7's were painted C&O dark blue with yellow trim but bore a South Shore herald on the flanks of their long hoods.

So that freight train numbers would better integrate with those of the passenger trains (where eastbound are odd numbered and westbound even) the 1500's were turned so that even-numbered units had their short hoods facing west and odd-numbered units, short hoods facing east. In June 1978 the railroad acquired three more used GP7's, from Florida East Coast, Nos. 614, 615 and 618. Except for painting out the FEC name on their flanks, none of these Geeps was repainted or renumbered into the South Shore's 1500 series.

Finally, in January 1981 South Shore took delivery of
Continued on page 104

Heading back to Gary and its resting place, the hulking 802 stamps across the IHB diamond and onto South Shore's own track (from K&E trackage) at State Line interlocking, Hammond, June 21, 1979.

Joe 802 is about to pull its loads from the Georgia Pacific lead back onto the westbound main to reassemble its train at Marshall siding on a sun-filled June day in 1979. (Right) Joe 803's proud nose looms large above photographer Kaplan as the unit awaits its biweekly servicing at Shops in June 1979; the unit was used to buck snow drifts the previous winter, hence the rusted nose door.

Scott Hartley

Above, an engineman's view from 802 at Shops in 1977. Engineer Dick Liebig (right) chats with the dispatcher in Michigan City during switching chores at the Georgia Pacific paper plant in Gary, June 21, 1979. (Left) Worn but nevertheless the symbol of excellence by its builder, the GE logo persists on the flank of 801 in June 1979.

GP38-2's 2005 and 2008 illustrate the new look of South Shore freight operations of the 1980's. The duo is eastbound at Miller on May 25, 1983.

ten brand new 2,000 h.p. GP38-2 diesels from EMD. Numbered 2000-2009 and painted Chessie yellow with dark blue trim and lettering, these units were deployed in the same east-west/odd-even orientation as the 1500's. Being the first purchase of new freight power since the 800's in 1949 and the first ordered specifically for the railroad since the 1000-series steeple-cabs in the 1930's, the GP38's represent a new era in freight muscle for the South Shore.

In a single stroke, the arrival of the 2000's permitted the railroad to retire the last of its electric motors and sell its aging fleet of second-hand diesels, which also had become unreliable and costly to maintain. Of the three 800's, the 801 (already partially dismantled for spare parts) was scrapped by Hyman-Michaels in Chicago in May 1981 whereas the 802 and 803 were donated for preservation to the B&O and Illinois Railway museums, respectively. GP7's 1501, 614, 615 and 618 were sold in May 1981 to D. A. Wilson of Ames, Iowa, who in turn resold the three ex-FEC units to Columbus & Greenville in Columbus, Miss. Numbers 1502-1508 were sent back to the C&O where they continued in service.

Thus for the first time since its purchase by Insull interests nearly sixty years ago, South Shore was beginning its 76th year with brand new, unified fleets of passenger and freight equipment. Not only has the presence of new equipment given the venerable interurban property a new image, but it also has bolstered employee and patron morale about the future of this unique institution.

Michigan City-Chicago train 274 streaks by unit coal train Extra 1504 West standing in the clear at Wagner siding on June 19, 1978. The second Geep, No. 614, is one of the GP7's acquired from Florida East Coast, and still painted in FEC colors.

(Left) Awaiting word from the dispatcher on the location of their next meet, Extra 2008 West is ready to depart Olive siding on March 28, 1982. (Above) Heavy lake-effect snow freckles a caboose hop crossing Amtrak and the former L&N (Monon) tracks at 10th and Huron in Michigan City, March 1982. (Below) A Burnham-bound coal train at Miller in March 1982.

9 A new interurban era

Since the South Shore line had conducted a profitable passenger service in the postwar period, why did its revenues decline to the point it needed governmental support to survive?

From a postwar peak of 6 million passengers in 1946, South Shore experienced a slow but steady decline in patronage until annual ridership in 1978 was less than 1.5 million. The reasons included: (1) the postwar resumption of private automobile production and purchase; (2) the postwar availability of tires and gasoline; (3) increased suburbanization; and (4) advances in highway construction, especially the development of urban and intercity freeways. Beginning in 1951, the declines in ridership resulted in operating losses. Profits from the railroad's freight operations were used to cover deficits from the passenger service until 1959, when the railroad overall experienced a minor net loss. From that point on the losses were reduced largely by cuts in passenger service in 1959, 1961 and 1964.

In 1969, freight profits again were unable to cover the losses. The net loss in 1970 amounted to $1 million and in 1971-72 the railroad sold off valuable real estate so that it could show a modest profit. By 1972, losses from the passenger service exceeded $2 million, and the number of passenger trains was slashed drastically.

Adding to the problems of decreased ridership was the deterioration of the passenger car fleet and the extra costs required to keep it operational. A fleet of new cars would have cost about $25 million, far more than South Shore and parent Chessie were willing or able to pay in 1972. At that point it was obvious that, if passenger service on the South Shore was to succeed, it would have to broaden its base of financial support.

Passage of the Urban Mass Transportation Assistance (UMTA) Act of 1964 established the precedent of federal aid for capital improvements and, after 1974, operating subsidies for transit agencies. Many properties availed themselves of this source of support. Unfortunately, because of its fiscal conservatism and deep-seated mistrust of governmental intervention in local affairs, the state of Indiana was very slow to tap such resources. It was only prompted to get involved by South Shore's formal threat of abandonment in late 1976. Many Hoosier citizens and legislators could not understand why the large and profitable parent Chessie system, owner of the CSS&SB since 1967, could not be expected to foot the bill for the losses and new cars.

As previously mentioned, South Shore had tried in the early 1970's to secure an UMTA grant for new rolling stock but Indiana could not supply the requisite matching funds. From 1973 on, the Illinois RTA supplied operating subsidies to South Shore in proportion to the number of passengers riding strictly within the boundaries of Illinois. Despite such outside support, the state of Indiana continued to drag its feet.

Frustrated by Indiana's apparent unwillingness to come to their aid, South Shore management finally threw down the gauntlet and filed an abandonment petition with the Interstate Commerce Commission (ICC) in November 1976 with the intention of discontinuing the passenger service on Dec. 8, 1976. To permit a proper investigation and allow time for abandonment hearings, the ICC deferred the service discontinuance until April 8, 1977. Following its investigation, the ICC determined there were reasons for saving the service, but gave the state of Indiana 10 months (until February 1978) to develop an appropriate support package. Fortunately, this time the state did respond and proceeded to pass legislation that would enable South Shore to obtain federal aid.

An important component of South Shore's salvation was the strong support voiced by both its riders and the public. People realized that, despite its deteriorated rolling stock, the line was an invaluable transportation resource that could be modernized at a fraction of the cost of building a new system, and that it was an historically unique institution that should be preserved. Grassroots citizens' organizations such as the Save Our South Shore league and South Shore Recreation were extraordinarily effective in drumming up public support for the railroad. To acquaint the non-commuting public with the South Shore as a valuable transportation artery, they ran excursions to special events such as jazz festivals in Chicago and recreation events in the Dunes and at Hudson Lake. In addition, they campaigned vigorously for the railroad with newspaper ads and lobbied legislators when critical bills were before the Indiana General Assembly.

While it is true that, compared with other parts of the country, Indiana had been slow to respond to mass transportation needs within its own borders, it did not wait for the South Shore crisis before dealing with the broader issues of transit in the state. As early as 1974 the federal government provided the state with a planning grant to inventory and evaluate its needs for public transportation. The inventory was conducted in 1975 by the Institute for Urban Transportation (IUT) of Indiana University at Bloomington. The inventory report recommended a program of state aid to mass transit in the form of monetary and technical assistance. At the same time, the Mass Transportation Study Commission (MTSC) appointed by the General Assembly made a study of the transportation situation and came to conclusions similar to those in the IUT report.

Responding to these recommendations, in 1975 the General Assembly created a state matching grant program for transit and allocated $2.5 million. It also formed the Public Transportation Advisory Committee (PTAC) to advise the governor on matters of public transportation and oversee the distribution of grant funds. The Institute for Urban Transportation, which

Framed in the gazebo at Gary's Gateway Park (next to the preserved Gary Land Office, the city's original building) is the new South Shore right-of-way through the city. Train 210 is at the east end of the new station on June 20, 1984; Broadway cuts under the station. Compare this scene with that at the top of page 100, which was photographed from essentially the same direction, though from on Broadway.

had carried out the initial study of state transportation resources in 1975, was chosen to administer the state's matching grant program. According to an allocation formula worked out by the IUT, $100,000 was to be made available to the South Shore for its operating subsidy. However, given the threats of discontinuance by Chessie, there was concern that South Shore might not be a wise investment of state funds that perhaps could be used more effectively on other, more viable transportation projects.

To determine more conclusively the potential of the South Shore in the northwestern Indiana transportation picture, in April 1976 the IUT received approval from the PTAC to conduct a detailed study of the South Shore corridor. The study, paid for by UMTA, was initiated in early 1977 and a draft of the results was completed by August of that year. The corridor study examined the following transportation options: (1) continuing South Shore passenger rail service; (2) reducing South Shore rail service and expanding other transportation modes (i.e., buses) to integrate with it; or (3) eliminating South Shore rail service altogether. Of all the options considered, the study determined that continuing rail service on the South Shore was the least costly, the most beneficial, the safest, the least polluting and would result in the least traffic congestion. The IUT study left little doubt that South Shore passenger service should be retained and improved.

In April 1977, responding to strong public pressure and to give evidence to both the ICC and South Shore of state efforts to save the passenger service, the General Assembly passed two bills that were critical to the interurban's survival. The first created the legal framework for the establishment of the Northern Indiana Commuter Transportation District (NICTD) to serve as a conduit for funding for the South Shore. The second appropriated $3.6 million as the state's share of a matching grant to replace the South Shore's rolling stock and refurbish the railroad's electrical system and car maintenance facilities. The state's contribution would be matched by those from each of the four northwestern Indiana counties served by the South Shore (from west to east, Lake, Porter, La Porte and St. Joseph) to provide 20 percent of a matching capital grant, with UMTA supplying the remaining 80 percent.

Under the provisions of the enabling legislation, Indiana commuter transportation districts such as NICTD were permitted to apply for and receive federal, state, county and municipal funds as well as private contribu-

The trackage at the new Gary station is similar to that of the old ground-level facility in that a holding spur for cut-off/add-on cars and turnback trains is situated between the two mains east of the depot. In this June 1984 scene, train 118 approaches; cars on spur will become train 218 an hour later.

tions and to use such funds for operating, capital and administrative expenses associated with assisting a commuter transportation system. While it was not empowered to levy taxes, NICTD was permitted to own or lease equipment and to set levels of service and fares.

Given the need for Indiana to demonstrate tangible accomplishments within the 10-month period set by the ICC, NICTD had its first meeting on June 27, 1977, a scant two months after passage of the enabling legislation. Membership of the district consisted of a board of trustees and its staff. The trustees included one representative from each of the four counties served by the South Shore and a trustee appointed by the governor to represent the interests of the state. To make more rapid progress, NICTD arranged to use members of the already established Northwestern Indiana Regional Planning Commission (NIRPC) for its staff. Members of NIRPC had been closely involved with the public campaign to save the South Shore. Because of their intimate knowledge of the region, their expertise would be of great value in helping to effect the railroad's renewal.

NICTD identified the three most urgent tasks to be accomplished: (1) Buy new rolling stock; (2) Refurbish the physical plant; and (3) provide operating subsidies. The capital improvements turned out to be easier to attain than the operating subsidies. Using data from the 1977 IUT South Shore corridor study as well as advice from independent consultants, NICTD applied to UMTA for capital funds. While funding for the grant would be delayed by difficulties with labor protection agreements and protracted negotiations over the operating subsidies, UMTA was willing to release funds for the initial engineering studies so some progress could be made.

The $67.5 million capital improvement program completed in 1983-84 involved not only the purchase of 44 new m.u. cars, 36 of which (Nos. 1-30, 39-44) are owned by NICTD and the other eight (Nos. 31-38) by Illinois RTA, but also installation of new, solid-state electrical switch gear in the substations between Michigan City and Chicago. Prior to their renovation, South Shore's 1500-volt d.c. electrical system would experience marked voltage drops, to values as low as 750-800 volts. The older m.u. cars, with less sophisticated technology, were able to operate under such low voltage conditions. The new cars, however, are designed to shut down when the voltage drops significantly.

Furthermore, preliminary engineering studies suggested that an additional substation was needed in the

vicinity of Hegewisch to effectively balance power loads in the busy, double-track section between Gary and Kensington. In this instance the RTA furnished the matching funds for its construction, along with those for a new substation at Jackson Street on the ICG in downtown Chicago.

Acquisition of the new cars also necessitated modernization of service facilities to maintain them. Not only did it require renovating the New Shop, but also adding more modern servicing equipment such as a wheel truing machine and drop table. Since the track layout at Shops had to be modified to accommodate the longer cars and a new car washer, it inspired a completely new design for the track arrangement in the Michigan City yard.

Attacking the third and knottiest facet of their mandate, the operating subsidies, the NICTD board finally achieved an operating agreement with the railroad in June 1978. While the monetary settlement for that first agreement (for the years 1975-78) fell far short of covering the full passenger deficit for those years, in subsequent years increased funding from the state covered a larger portion of the losses. In 1982 an agreement was reached that compensated the South Shore for 100 percent of its operating losses and provided the railroad with the kind of multi-year agreement it required.

Revenues for NICTD's increased subsidy payments have come from a variety of state sources, plus a 50 percent contribution from UMTA. For example, in 1979 the General Assembly and the governor established the Commuter Rail Service Fund (CRSF). Its source is an indefinite situs distribution property tax on railroad car leasing companies. The tax raises about $1.5-1.7 million per year and represented the first source of dedicated funding for the South Shore's operating subsidy. Additional funding came in 1980 from the Public Mass Transportation Fund (PMTF) whereby 0.95 percent of Indiana's sales tax is deposited with PMTF. From this source NICTD could count on an additional $0.5 million per year. Subsequent legislation provided NICTD with additional funds by giving them bonding authority as well as authority to receive property taxes that had been

Above right, conductor Mike Thomas gives engineer Dave Arndt the highball as train 118 departs Gary on June 20, 1984, during the first week of the new depot. (Center right) New Gary ticket office. (Right) Finding the old station closed, a family of South Shore patrons puzzles where to catch the trains. The view is from the new elevated station.

collected from the South Shore but redirected to NICTD. These various tax sources enabled NICTD to supply a more satisfactory level of compensation to the South Shore without relying on local taxes.

In the seven years since its inception, NICTD has developed from a funding agency to an operating agency increasingly involved in the day-to-day operations of the railroad. Not only is it responsible for scheduling service and establishing fare levels, but also for supervising passenger car maintenance and substation repair.

While the first and most crucial phases of South Shore's physical renewal have been completed, NICTD has a host of projects—some already scheduled and others on the drawing boards—that will further alter the appearance and nature of the South Shore's service. One of the most immediate projects is a joint program with the RTA to reconstruct the South Shore's terminal at Randolph St. in Chicago. The present facility, with its curving tracks and platforms, does not adequately accommodate the longer cars of the new fleet. The plan calls for straightening this trackage and the platforms serving it and reducing the number of tracks from five to four. The tracks will be served by two high-level platforms rather than the three now in service. Such realignments will be accompanied by a modernization of this outmoded facility.

At the eastern end of the line there are plans for changes in the South Bend terminal that are even more radical. This west-side station will be relocated to the nearby Michiana Regional Airport. South Shore trains will reach the planned intermodal terminal by a relocated freight lead. This terminal relocation would encourage greater use of the South Bend airport, especially by those travelers to northwestern Indiana who could fly to South Bend and use South Shore trains to reach their final destinations. Given the congested air traffic at Chicago's O'Hare airport, this could have considerable appeal if the South Shore could schedule more frequent service to South Bend.

In late 1984 a new station was to be erected at Indiana highway 49 and the South Shore railroad about a mile west of the Tremont stop. The new location will more effectively serve riders from the community of Chesterton to the south and provide direct access to the main entrance of the Indiana Dunes National Lakeshore Park. This new station is to be done in the Insull-Spanish design similar to that at Beverly Shores. With the opening of this new Dune facility, Tremont was to be closed.

Following renovation of the substations in the more heavily trafficked sector west of Michigan City, there are plans to refurbish those between Michigan City and South Bend. There also are plans to weld the rail in this eastern sector.

Some time before the end of the 1980s, improvements will be made to the catenary system along the length of the line. Freezing temperatures during severe winters have caused breaks in the wire, with attendant disruptions of passenger service. One way to reduce such problems might be the use of constant—tension catenary similar to that installed in Philadelphia.

NICTD already has instituted a modest but effective marketing program to stimulate off-peak ridership on the South Shore during weekdays and, especially, on weekends. NICTD has promoted South Shore travel to special events such as an ethnic festival in South Bend, baseball and football games in Chicago, summer trips to the Dunes and cross country skiing near Hudson Lake in the winter. Ultimately NICTD hopes to improve the quantity of service offered by the railroad with a goal of staggered hourly levels of service to South Bend and Gary, like the South Shore offered in the postwar period.

It would be nice to conclude this book with an upbeat view that the recent renovation of the South Shore means its future is all rosy. But there are still many unsettled problems. Even the recent re-equipment of the passenger service has produced problems. For example, the new fleet of modern cars has produced marked increases in ridership. As a result, certain rush hour trains are terribly overcrowded, unable to accommodate the increases in patronage the new equipment was supposed to encourage. Some of these problems might be resolved in the short term by equipment shuffles that would allow certain trains up to eight cars. But if increases in ridership continue, it may necessitate the purchase of additional cars, including motors and trailers.

Hanging like a cloud over all these plans and goals is the question of continuing funding for the South Shore, especially with regard to operating subsidies. NICTD has been successful in meeting these expenses by a clever combination of taxes and resources from state and local governments combined with a 50 percent contribution from UMTA. However, the mid-1980's fiscal

The new era of the South Shore, ushered in with the new equipment, also meant new structures such as the substation at Hegewisch, Ill. Train 212 is bound for Chicago on June 20, 1984.

The new drop-table facility on track 6 at the New Shop, installed as part of the general capital improvement grant, will allow shopmen to change trucks without having to jack up cars.

Interior of new car-wash building at Michigan City shows control center at left (glassed in area) and brushes. Enclosed facilities will permit year-round car washing.

The carmen's building (left in photo) and the car-wash building (at right) are the newest additions to shop facilities in Michigan City.

atmosphere in Washington indicates that some federal operating subsidies might be cut as much as 38 percent, necessitating increased compensation at the state and local levels.

The legality of one of the major sources of state funding for the South Shore deficits, the Commuter Rail Service Fund (CRSF), has been challenged by the Private Truck Council of America because of Indiana's institution of a similar indefinte situs tax on motor carriers in the state. In April 1983, a Circuit Court judge ruled this tax was unconstitutional and that it could not be collected. The state is appealing the Circuit Court's decision, but if upheld, it could be a disaster for NICTD because the tax supplies the South Shore with a major portion of its subsidy.

One potential source of long-term funding that has been explored is NICTD's purchase of the South Shore from Chessie, using profits from the freight business to subsidize the losses from the passenger service. For several years, the Chessie system has indicated a desire to sell the South Shore because the interurban property no longer fits into its development plans. Such a move

by NICTD is fraught with legal complications, including questions about the long-term profitability of the freight business and whether a public transit agency should be in the freight business. A state purchase could offer a solution to the funding problem, however, and the Indiana General Assembly has provided the legislation to permit it.

Regardless of what the future holds for the South Shore, a broader perspective shows it to have been an organization of extraordinary resiliency throughout its 76-year history. Every time it seemed to be counted down and out, it sprang back with renewed vigor. There is no reason to think it will not exhibit the same degree of adaptability in the future. Even though the problem of funding may cloud its future, the strong declaration of public support and extensive re-investment in its physical plant suggest the citizens of northwestern Indiana will make every effort to see that their investment is protected. Moreover, the South Shore's unique status as the last interurban in the United States will undoubtedly give greater impetus for its preservation and use in the future.

Acknowledgments

My interest in the South Shore Line spans nearly 35 years and was nurtured by the extraordinary kindness and generosity of its employees. Foremost in this regard was R. E. Jamieson, Passenger Traffic Manager from the Insull era until the early 1960's. Not only did "Jamie" provide me with ample literature and opportunities to visit the property when I was a teenager, but in 1953 he even accompanied me on train from Randolph Street to Michigan City just so I could have a long-desired front platform ride with the engineer.

Such a tradition of kindness has continued on the railroad to this day and has been expressed by the help its management and employees have provided me in all phases of the preparation of this book. For example, Albert W. Dudley, President and General Manager during Chessie ownership, not only afforded me unparalleled opportunities to photograph the line and its facilities, but also lent insight to its freight traffic development. Richard D. Shipley, Superintendent of Transportation and Casualty Prevention, was equally helpful in describing the details of current freight traffic patterns. Richard D. Bunton, Director of Passenger and Administrative Services, not only provided an invaluable overview of the South Shore's corporate organization and function but also read and critiqued an early draft of the text. Charles F. Mulrenan of the engineering department provided a wealth of information on the railroad's infrastructure, and especially the latest construction developments and plans. John R. Dukehart, Superintendent of the Mechanical Department, examined portions of the text relative to his area and gave a detailed account of the modernization of the New Shop building. Dave Arndt, engineer and longtime friend, not only read and critiqued the text but also supplied me with invaluable details on the South Shore's operating procedures. Finally, Dan S. Bechly, Engineer-Structures on the Illinois Central Gulf Railroad was very helpful with information on trackage and grades on the ICG's suburban electrified district.

A special vote of thanks goes to Daniel J. Gornstein, equipment engineer with NICTD. Dan not only provided technical information on the new South Shore cars but also uncovered new data on the car-ordering sequences by the Insull management.

I am also indebted to John Paul Laue, Marketing Coordinator for NICTD; George Krambles, former Executive Director of the Chicago Transit Authority; Professor John C. Spychalski of the College of Business Administration, Pennsylvania State University; and Ms. Eleanor Crump, my personal editor, for their critical reading of the text and their helpful suggestions for its improvement.

George M. Smerk, Professor of Transporation in the Business School at Indiana University, Bloomington, and the Governor's Appointee to the NICTD Board of Trustees, deserves a special note of appreciation. Throughout the course of this project he served as a continuing source of encouragement, providing sources of information on the day-to-day changes in policy and operations during this dynamic period of transition in the road's history. Moreover, he not only read and criticized several drafts of the text but also provided invaluable resources for the final chapter on the public rescue of the passenger service.

This book's striking imagery is due to the efforts of a host of dedicated photographers who have recorded the railroad in good weather and bad during this important phase of its history. They include Phil Borleske, Don Crimmin, Chuck Crouse, Ed DeRouin, Don Ellison, Lou Gerard, Denny Hamilton, Scott Hartley, Tom Post and Mike Schafer. I am indebted to them all for their contributions and for the opportunity to display their artistry in this work.

Finally, I wish to express my gratitude to PTJ Publisher Kevin McKinney and his fine staff for their effective collaboration and encouragement during the course of this project. Kevin P. Keefe and Mike Schafer, in particular, were the sources of the idea for this publication. Their great skills in editing and book design helped to transform a rudimentary text and set of photographs into a polished publication of great visual appeal.

Donald R. Kaplan
Kensington, Calif.
1984

DUNELAND ELECTRIC
From the publishers of PASSENGER TRAIN JOURNAL and PROTOTYPE MODELER

PUBLISHED BY
PTJ Publishing, Inc., Homewood, Ill.

PUBLISHER
Kevin McKinney

PROJECT MANAGER AND EDITOR
Kevin P. Keefe

EDITORIAL ASSISTANCE
John H. Kuehl, Kevin McKinney, Mike Schafer

BOOK LAYOUT AND ART PRODUCTION
Kevin P. Keefe, Allen Ambrosini, Mike Schafer

TYPESETTING
Publishers Studio, Waukesha, Wis.

HALFTONES, COLOR SEPARATIONS AND IMAGE ASSEMBLY
Jim Walter Graphic Arts, Beloit, Wis.

PRINTING
Walsworth Publishing Co., Marceline, Mo.